THE THEORY OF

FINANCIAL MANAGEMENT

EZRA SOLOMON

THE THEORY OF
FINANCIAL
MANAGEMENT

 NEW YORK AND LONDON 1963
COLUMBIA UNIVERSITY PRESS

TO JANET

FOREWORD

Professor Solomon's book is one of two experimental volumes prepared at the request of The Ford Foundation as part of its program
to encourage new directions in business education. The other experimental volume, Marketing: Executive and Buyer Behavior, was
written by Professor John A. Howard of the University of Pitts-
burgh.

In the United States, business education has undergone a far-
reaching transformation during the past ten years. The predom-
inantly vocational orientation of the past is rapidly giving way to
professional curricula of a more scientific nature. This transformation has been characterized by intensive application to managerial problems of the underlying disciplines—the social sciences,
modern mathematics and statistics; a greater emphasis on analysis rather than description in the teaching process; and the development of fundamental research on the business process.

In order to speed the diffusion of these new directions throughout the nation's six hundred schools and departments of business
administration, the Foundation has supported a variety of special
activities. Among these efforts are "new developments" summer
seminars for teachers of business conducted by the Carnegie Institute of Technology and the Universities of California (Berkeley)
and Chicago; an Institute of Basic Mathematics for Application to
Business conducted for a year at Harvard and M. I. T. and suc-
ceeded by summer programs at eight other universities; and business school deans' seminars in modern research developments.

As a natural extension of the "new developments" seminars,
it was suggested that the Foundation encourage the preparation of
written materials to provide teachers throughout the country with
readier access to recent advances in particular areas of business
administration. The two fields selected for the first experimental

volumes were finance and marketing. We are grateful to Professors Howard and Solomon for undertaking the difficult assignment of preparing the monographs. These books, it should be emphasized, are not intended as texts for students, whether undergraduate or graduate. The books are directed toward teachers of marketing and finance in the hope that they will contribute toward the enrichment of their teaching. Needless to say, the use to which a teacher can put these studies is a highly individual matter. It will depend heavily on his own background and interests as well as the nature and level of courses for which he is responsible.

DYKE BROWN
Vice President
The Ford Foundation

PREFACE

Recent contributions in the field of financial management have made the subject broader and more analytical. Today academic as well as professional discussions on the problem of committing and raising capital funds on behalf of an individual enterprise contain a much larger component of theory than they did in the past.

This book examines this emerging component of analysis and its relevance for managerial decisions on three basic issues: the volume of assets to be held by an enterprise, the structure of these holdings, and the composition of financing to be used.

All three questions have been the subject of vigorous analytical inquiry during the past few years. This inquiry has already had an important impact on financial thinking and practice and it promises to have an equally significant effect on the scope and content of academic courses in the field.

What follows is an introduction to current thinking in the field, written as simply as the subject allows. It is not put forward as an original contribution to theory nor as a documented critique of the literature in the field. I have borrowed freely from the growing body of analytical writing currently being addressed to fundamental, but long neglected, issues in financial management. However the literature in this area is recent and controversial and important segments are marked by contradiction and confusion. In developing an integrated statement on financial issues and their solutions it has been necessary to pick and choose, to simplify, and even to reargue many points in the interest of clarity.

The treatment of the subject is textual in style, but not in coverage. I have made no attempt to include the topics traditionally surveyed by works in financial management, but have tried only to provide an underlying framework of analysis and theory which

might serve to unify the existing body of descriptive and case materials contained in these works.

For decades, the structure of academic work in corporation
and business finance has followed a pattern which was laid down
very early in its history. One of the first texts in the field, published in 1910, states: "Corporation... finance aims to explain
and illustrate the methods employed in the promotion, capitalization, financial management, consolidation and reorganization of
business corporations."* Texts which have dominated the field
since that time have not parted greatly from this structure, but
have continued the pattern of a heavily descriptive content built
around the major financing episodes in the life cycle of a hypothetical enterprise.

The structure I have used cuts across the traditional pattern.
It deals in relatively abstract and theoretical terms with general
and interrelated issues applicable to all forms of financial decisions: How much capital should an enterprise commit? In what
form should the commitments be made? How should the required
funds be raised? All are facets of a basic problem in valuation
under conditions of uncertainty—set within a framework of con-
straints imposed by the market for goods, services, and capital.
The answers to these questions are relevant to virtually all of the
component segments of the traditional structure of the subject,
including those newer aspects which have been added since 1910,
such as expansion, merger, working capital, management, and
social control.

A number of possible reasons can be advanced for restructuring the subject of financial management in accordance with the
dictates of analytical sequence rather than of descriptive content.
My own attempt to do so was provoked by the task of designing a
course in financial management at the Massachusetts Institute of
Technology for a group of senior executives, most of whom already knew a great deal about the mechanics of company financing,
none of whom were particularly interested in a detailed description of legal and accounting processes by which corporations are
born, marry, divorce, or die, and all of whom were concerned
with the financial issues involved in managing an ongoing enterprise.

*Edward S. Mead, <u>Corporation Finance</u> (New York, D. Appleton and
Company, Inc., 1910), p. viii.

Since that time I have had the opportunity to use the analytically structured approach put forward in this book in teaching groups of students, teachers, and executives, for the purpose of in-company discussions and training programs comprising all levels of management, and also to teach in management programs abroad.

This experience convinced me that the subject of financial management contains an interesting and important component of theory which is of direct relevance to the practical art of managing the financial affairs of an enterprise. I have also become convinced that the small but growing body of deduction and analysis which comprises this component provides a vehicle for academic instruction which is more suitable for university-level courses than that provided by the traditional structure of specialized and segmented description.

I am grateful to the Ford Foundation which provided the stimulus, the opportunity, and the funds required to record these ideas systematically. I owe at least an equal debt to colleagues in the field from whom many of the ideas themselves are derived, in particular to Joel Dean, whose pioneer work in capital budgeting in 1951 ushered in much of the present emphasis on this subject; to James Lorie, Harry Roberts, and Joel Segall at the University of Chicago; to Eli Shapiro, David Durand, and Myron Gordon at MIT; to John Lintner, Pearson Hunt, and Paul Cook at Harvard; to Fred Weston and Jack Hirshleifer at UCLA; and to Franco Modigliani and Merton Miller, until recently at the Carnegie Institute of Technology. None of them will agree with everything in this book, some will disagree strongly with parts of it, but all will find one or more segments that lean heavily on their own work in the field.

The principal focus of what follows is on normative theory as it applies to an individual company—a conceptual scheme of decisions to be made by financial management and appropriate ways of making them. This is of course only one point of departure. In addition to normative theory we need concrete applications to specific problems, documentation of how firms actually conduct their financial affairs, either individually or in large groups, and finally, a framework of positive theory which covers economic interrelations in the capital market as a whole including both suppliers and users of funds. But for the present, a major gap in the field is the lack of normative theory of financial management at the

level of the individual firm, and it is toward closing this gap that
the contents of this book are directed.

Ezra Solomon

Stanford University
September, 1961

CONTENTS

I. THE SCOPE OF THE FINANCE FUNCTION

How should the scope of financial management be defined for purposes of academic study? There is no clear-cut answer to this question but rather a whole range of possible approaches.

One apparently straightforward approach is to define it as things done by the most obviously financial officer in any company, the treasurer. The trouble with this empirical definition is that the responsibilities carried by company treasurers vary quite widely from one organization to another While it is true that the treasurer always performs financial functions of some kind it is also clear that important aspects of financial management are frequently handled outside his office. Thus, the responsibility for basic financial decisions might rest in one company with a committee of the board of directors, in another with the president, in others at the vice-presidential level, with or without the designation "financial," and in still others with the controller. Given this wide diversity of organizational practices, the core of financial functions always to be found attaching to the office of treasurer consists only of routine responsibilities that are better classified as administrative functions incidental to finance rather than as financial management proper. These incidental functions— the receipt, disbursement, protection, and custody of funds and securities, the preparation of confidential payrolls, the supervision of bond registrations and transfers, the management of real estate and personal property taxes, the negotiation and placement of insurance, are important, but they hardly involve decisions in financial management and there is general agreement that they do not warrant study in a university curriculum.

Nor is it possible to bypass the difficulty involved in the empirical approach by defining the scope of financial management in terms of the observable decisions made by "financial managers"

rather than by treasurers. The financial manager is not an inde-
pendently identifiable officer within most organizations. Indeed
there is such a diversity of organizational practices in existence
the person or persons who make the principal financial decisions
within an enterprise can be located only after the scope and nature of these decisions have first been defined. In short, direct
observation of practices in the field can be most useful in help-
ing us to select from among alternative a priori definitions of
the scope of financial decisions, but it cannot provide an independent answer to the definitional question.[1]

Alternative Approaches

A priori definitions of the scope of financial management fall
into three broad groupings. One considers that finance is concerned with cash, and that since nearly every business transac-
tion involves cash directly or indirectly, finance is concerned with
everything that takes place in the conduct of a business. Most writers agree that such a definition is too broad to be meaningful.

At the other extreme is the relatively narrow definition that
financial management is concerned with raising and administering
funds used in an enterprise. This is the approach that has traditionally dominated academic work in financial management.
Like the dictionary definition of the word "finance," it centers
almost exclusively on the procurement of funds, widened of course
to cover a discussion of the instruments, institutions, and practices through which funds are obtained and of the legal and accounting relationships between a company and its sources of
funds, including the redistribution of income and assets among
these sources. In economic terms this approach to financial management assumes that the demand for capital funds and the expenditure decisions which give rise to this demand are determined
elsewhere within an organization and ascribes to financial policy
only the task of determining how these funds can best be raised
from the combination of sources available.

The third approach is that financial management is properly
viewed as an integral part of over-all management rather than
as a staff speciality concerned with fund-raising operations. In
this broader view the central issue of financial policy is the wise
use of funds, and the central process involved is a rational matching of the advantages of potential uses against the cost of alter-

native potential sources so as to achieve the broad financial
goals which an enterprise sets for itself. The underlying fund-
using proposals which originate within the operating departments
of an enterprise are still assumed as given. So are present and
prospective conditions in technology and in the markets for goods,
services, and capital. Given these data, the function of financial
management is to review and control decisions to commit or re-
commit funds to new or ongoing uses. Thus, in addition to raising funds, financial management is directly concerned with production, marketing, and other functions within an enterprise
whenever decisions are made about the acquisition or destruction
of assets.

This broader view of the scope of the finance function is
emerging rapidly in recent academic and professional thinking
in the field—and it is the one adopted in this book. However the
point of view itself is by no means new. Indeed, among the best
statements of this approach to the finance function is one written
in 1925 for the opening number of the American Management
Association's Financial Executives' Series. It reads as follows:

"The job of the financial executive demands that he phase in
his viewpoints with the operating executive in each division of
his organization, compelling him as well to view every problem
presented, not only from the standpoint of his ability to finance
the project, but also from the perspective of the operator, who
considers it primarily from the standpoint of facilitating more
efficient operations and production. To analyze the increase or
reduction in expense, to estimate properly the probable increase
in earnings and to weigh the operating advantages incident to the
completion of the project against the cost of capital to finance it,
the determination of his ability to provide such capital and the
methods with which he will provide it are some of the problems
of the financial executive. Increase in efficiency of operations
must be encouraged, cash and credit must be conserved and his
conclusion and concurrence must find the happy medium, which
does not always exist, between the two viewpoints that focus on
the proposal. To accede on one hand, without proper regard for
the factors which are his own particular problems, may bring
embarrassment and failure; and to veto, on the other hand, without seeming to lend a willing hand and without the ability and en-
deavor to point out strong reasons, with logic, diplomacy and tact,
may destroy the spirit of cooperation desirable at all times, kill

the initiative of the operator, still his ingenuity and impair the possibility of efficient coordination of the numerous departments of the business.

"The fundamental duty of a financial executive demands a constant realization of his responsibilities to the owners of the enterprise. A proper appreciation of this primary responsibility will insist that invested capital shall bring a fair return, that additional capital shall be provided for necessary expansions to produce the same result. In order to successfully administer these obligations, additional functions are created. A satisfactory credit position must be established with banks, investment houses and other financial agencies and a thorough understanding should be had of the various methods of financing, giving proper regard to the fact that banking credit is available only for current transactions and that capital expenditures must ultimately be provided through issues of stocks or bonds. To the financial executive whose organization is receiving the benefits of customer or employee ownership there is added the duty of assisting in the promotion and furtherance of good will among the company's employees, customers and friends leading to the creation of an ever-increasing number of satisfied partners. This is accomplished through the distribution of understandable and reliable information together with the maintenance of a proper relationship with these people as security holders. In this case the financial executive is also responsible for the initiation and maintenance of proper security sales policies whether distribution is effected through employee campaigns, through full-time sales force carried by the company, or through investment bankers".[2]

The Traditional View of Finance

Although the broader definition of the scope of finance was put forward during the nineteen-twenties, little was done to amend the subject matter of academic work in financial management along the lines implied by this approach.[3] Instead, the mainstream of academic writing and teaching followed the scope and pattern suggested by the narrower and by now "traditional" definition of the finance function. Only in recent years has the subject developed a content based on the broader or "modern" definition of its scope. It is useful to explore the reasons for the long dominance of the narrower approach and the factors underlying the recent reemergence of the broader alternative.

Financial management, or corporation finance, as it was then more generally called, emerged as a separate branch of economics during the early years of the present century. At that time the principal emphasis in economics was on institutions and institutional arrangements. The economics of the individual firm had not yet been developed as a focal point of inquiry. Within this general context, the purpose of corporation finance was to describe and to document the rapidly evolving complex of capital market institutions, instruments, and practices.

This pattern was already established by the early 1920s, when academic work in business administration, and hence in finance, developed on a large scale. It was reinforced by two factors. One was the wide growth of security ownership after World War I and the accompanying growth of public interest in corporations, their securities, and the network through which they obtained funds from the public. The other was the publication in 1920 of Arthur S. Dewing's The Financial Policy of Corporations. This book established the existing pattern of treatment in the field even more firmly by providing a definitive and scholarly text around which teachers could build their courses, and the book itself dominated academic works in the field for decades.[4]

The traditional treatment of finance did not go unchallenged. Indeed, it was criticized more or less continually throughout the period of its dominance. But what was questioned was not so much the definition of the finance function on which it was based, as matters of treatment and emphasis.[5] In particular, critical attention was directed to four related aspects of the traditional treatment.

The first is that the traditional approach treats the entire subject of finance from the point of view of the investment banker rather than that of the financial decision-maker within an enterprise. This criticism is generally accompanied by a suggestion that at least part of the content of finance should be "from the inside looking out rather than from the outside looking in."[6]

The second is that traditional treatment placed altogether too much emphasis on corporation finance and too little on the financing problems of noncorporate enterprises.

The third is that the sequence of treatment was built too closely around the episodic but infrequent phases during the life cycle of a hypothetical corporation during which external financial relations happen to be dominant. The argument in this connection is that overemphasis on matters like promotion, incorporation,

merger, consolidation, recapitalization, and reorganization left
too little room for the problems of a normal growing company.

Finally, critics questioned the heavy emphasis which the traditional approach placed on long-term financing instruments and
problems and its corresponding lack of emphasis on problems of
working capital management.

All of the implied suggestions, but particularly the last one,
brought about a continuing change in treatment and emphasis. At
the same time the increased use of cases as a medium of instruction provided analytical accents which served to leaven the heavily descriptive tone of academic work in this field. But in spite
of these amendments dissatisfaction with the present content and
quality of academic course work in financial mangement remains,
traceable largely to its lack of analytical substance and a conse-
quent overemphasis on descriptive detail.[7]

The New Approach

The basic problem with financial management as an academic
discipline is not entirely a matter of treatment or emphasis. It
has its roots in the fact that the subject has continued to address
itself to issues involved in the procurement of funds. As long as
academic work in financial management is confined to the process
of raising funds to finance expenditure-decisions that have already
been made elsewhere, it cannot and does not deal explicitly with
such questions as: Should an enterprise commit capital funds to
certain purposes? Do the expected returns meet financial standards of performance? How should these standards be set and what
is the cost of capital funds to the enterprise? How does this cost
vary with the mixture of financing methods used?

These questions lie at the very heart of sound financial management. What is more, an explicit analysis of these central
issues is necessary before any defensible answer can be given
even to the narrower and more traditional question of how required funds should be raised. Unless it is approached as part of
the overall financial problem of capital allocation, the answer to
the question, "How should a company raise funds?" invariably
devolves into the familiar description of instruments, practices,
rules, recipes, and observations built around chapter headings
that have changed little in fifty years.

Although bypassed in the traditional literature, what I have

called the central issues of financial management have become
the subject of considerable attention, interest, and controversy in
recent years. The problems themselves are by no means new.
Business firms have always had to make decisions about capital
allocation: how much capital to invest, what assets to acquire, and
what the composition of financing should be. Directly or indirectly,
those managing an enterprise have had to select the size and structure of its assets and liabilities and the rate of change in these
elements. What is new is the modern interest in developing an
explicit and systematic basis for making these decisions and the
associated attempt to make positive use of the capital allocation
process as a formal framework for achieving long-range goals.

This interest in the development of the systematic approaches
to capital management and financial planning has been stimulated
by a number of developments since World War II. In the United
States, rapid economic growth and swift changes in technology and
markets, together with rising competitive pressures, created a
situation which required a careful and systematic rationing of capital funds among alternative uses. Developments in other fields,
notably in the measurement and projection of economic data and
in the control and prediction of operating costs, have made it increasingly feasible for managements to install systems of capital
rationing and budgeting geared more closely to relevant information. At the same time the growth of special skills and departments
within decentralized or decentralizing enterprises has made it
necessary for management to develop a central mechanism for
dealing with capital investment and reinvestment decisions, and
to base these decisions on a defensible and understandable system
of analysis.

Scholars and practitioners who faced the task of establishing
applicable criteria for the wise use of funds found even the most
basic questions surrounded by difficult and unsolved issues. How
should the cost of capital funds be measured? How should capital-
using proposals be assayed? How does financing policy influence
the cost of capital? Surprisingly enough, these issues had received virtually no attention either in the field of financial management or in the main body of economic theory.

The recent interest in these issues has not been confined to the
United States or to private profit-seeking enterprises. Decisions
about many types of public-sector investment involve similar
questions of capital allocation and capital cost.[8] Even the cen-

trally planned economics, which had earlier abolished "profitability" and "interest" as inventions of the capitalist devil, have
begun to reintroduce these concepts in disguised form as guides
to the more efficient utilization of scarce funds among competing
uses. In doing so they too have wrestled with a basic issue of
financial management: how should capital costs be measured and
used in making optimal investment decisions?[9]

Widespread interest in the problem of capital allocation has
given rise to a vigorous discussion of these issues during the past
few years, in both academic and professional circles. In the
course of these discussions a significant body of analysis has
been developed around the central questions of financial policy.
While many aspects of the problem are still the subject of debate,
the ideas put forward in the literature, especially since 1955, provide most of the elements required for a theory of financial management in the broader definition of the term.

The Content of the New Approach

If the scope of financial management is redefined to cover decisions about both the use and the acquisition of funds it is clear
that the principal content of the subject should be concerned with
how financial management should make judgments about whether
an enterprise should hold, reduce, or increase its investment in
all forms of assets that require company funds. This in turn requires a defensible basis for answering three questions:
   1. What specific assets should an enterprise acquire?
   2. What total volume of funds should an enterprise commit?
   3. How should the funds required be financed?

These questions are closely interrelated. The total volume of
finance will be influenced by the kinds of investment opportunities
available as well as by conditions affecting the sources from which
financing is derived. Similarly, the cost and availability of funds
depend in part on the quantity and quality of investment purposes
for which they will be used. In other words, the three questions
outlined above are really three facets of a single underlying question and in practice they must be solved simultaneously.

An alternative way of stating the content of these three related
questions is as follows:
   1. How large should an enterprise be, and how fast should it
grow?

2. In what form should it hold its assets?

3. What should be the composition of its liabilities?

A rational basis for answering these questions has several prerequisites:

The first is the establishment of an explicit goal towards which financial management must be directed. The goal which is generally put forward is the maximization of the present worth of those who own the enterprise—although this is frequently stated in terms of the maximization of long-run earnings. While this is the most frequently cited objective it warrants careful restatement because there is some confusion about what the goal itself means in operating terms, about its desirability, as well as about a potential conflict between it and other specific goals and policies to which management might wish to direct itself.

The second is the establishment of a systematic and correct basis for directing funds into and through an enterprise so as to achieve long-run financial goals. This contains two component elements.

One is an organizational framework within which relevant information on all available courses of investment and financing can be assembled. On the investment side this includes not only proposals for the acquisition of plants and equipment but all proposals using company funds for existing or new operations, and covering both fixed assets and working capital assets. The use of a central capital budget as the formal framework within which management makes and expresses its decisions is not yet universal practice, but it is growing considerably in importance, relative to the alternative procedure of item-by-item decisions made at separate points within a company and at separate times. The extension of a central capital allocation framework to cover the holding and acquisition of working assets such as inventory, accounts receivable, and research programs is still relatively rare. However, for purposes of academic discussion financial management must be concerned with all uses of funds, regardless of the form they take.

The second element is a defensible body of analysis which will provide the operating criteria and objectives that best accomplish the over-all goal or goals established earlier.

One such criterion is the basic standard of financial performance which must be established as a yardstick against which all uses of funds can be assayed. How should an enterprise go about

the task of establishing such a yardstick in a world in which funds
can be obtained in many different ways, ranging from debt issues,
at one extreme, to retained earnings, at the other? What is the
correct standard of performance for investments whose yields
are uncertain in varying degrees? The problem of finding a measurable answer which is always consonant with the financial goal
of maximizing present worth is one of the central issues of modern financial analysis. The subject of financing is equally concerned with the complementary problem of measuring the investment worth of potential capital uses correctly, understandably,
and in a form that lends itself to the subsequent task of comparing
these measures against established standards of performance.

The third prerequisite is the establishment of a defensible
approach to the problem of selecting an optimum combination of
the many kinds of financing available to the modern enterprise.
This approach must take into account the cost of different sources
of funds, the effect of financing through one source on the cost of
other sources, and prospective changes in these costs and their
relationships.

The preceding survey of the proper content of financial management gives it a considerably broader content than that envisaged
by the traditional treatment of the field. But this does not mean
the finance function is concerned with every aspect of business
operations. A large group of business decisions do not involve
changes in the use of funds, and these lie outside the orbit of financial management even though they may have important consequences for the profitability of the enterprise. It is useful to
think of these as "technical" of nonfinancial decisions. Some
examples of technical decisions are pricing decisions; changes in
marketing and advertising techniques that do not involve a change
in the annual advertising budget; decisions about production processes which are not accompanied by a rise in aggregate inventory
or equipment; decisions on organizational, administrative, and
employee relationships. Many of these affect the size and timing
of future fund flows, but they do not involve a current change in
the volume of investment.

It might also be asked whether there is any difference between
the suggested definition of financial planning and the concept of
profit planning that has received so much attention in the recent
managerial literature. The two areas of thinking are close in several respects. In fact, it has been suggested that the subject of

profit planning is a component part of financial management in its broader sense.[10] The distinction between the two largely concerns the level at which it occurs. Profit planning takes place at the divisional or plant level and it focuses principally on current operations. Financial planning is part of general management. It is concerned not so much with operating details as with the relationship between the capital markets, on the one hand, and the use of funds within an enterprise, on the other. In fact, in the broadest sense the function of the financial viewpoint is to serve as the point of contact between the uses of funds within an enterprise and its sources of funds. Profit planning is and should be concerned with all decisions affecting profitability whether or not they require a net increase or decrease in the usage of funds. Financial management as we have defined it is directly involved only when the stock of assets and hence the use of funds is increased or decreased.

Relationship to Other Fields

Some of the developments associated with the broader approach to financial management have already been incorporated in segments of recent academic texts in the field. The next few years are likely to see their more complete adoption as the core of standard academic curricula in management. If this development does occur the already changing pattern of academic work in finance will shift more rapidly in several directions.

The optimal use of funds—optimal with respect to the volume composition, and timing of both source and uses—will replace the process of fund raising as the central issue of the subject matter. This change in scope will bring corresponding changes in content and emphasis.

The principal content will be an exercise in inference rather than in observation; a way of thinking about these central issues rather than a detailed description of the procedures and practices that relate a firm to its sources of financing. In short, the discussion of financial decisions will be based more on deduction than on observations about past practices.

The traditional approach has placed its main emphasis on the liabilities side of the balance sheet. It will give way to one that concentrates on the relationship between the profitability of holding assets and the cost of incurring liabilities in order to do so.

Finally, the specialized description of corporate law and accounting as they relate to financing episodes which now provides
the framework of treatment will be replaced by a generalized
treatment of these episodes as special aspects of the basic problems of financial evaluation.

How does the principal content of the broader approach to financial management compare with the process of financial management as it is viewed by practicing executives? The evidence
suggests that there is close correspondence between the two.
Aspects of finance which occupy a central place within the broad
approach—long-range planning, capital, and long-term budgeting—
are rated high in importance by financial managers.[11]

The relation of the new approach to financial management to
other segments of academic thinking is harder to define. Two major sectors of subject matter are involved. One is economic theory, particularly those branches of it dealing with the microeco-
nomic theory of the firm and the theory of capital. The other is
the traditional body of knowledge on corporation finance and financial institutions. In a broad sense, the theory of financial
management bridges the gap between these two sectors and lies
midway between them with respect to both content and level of
abstraction.

As far as economics is concerned, the theory of financial management can be viewed as an extension of the theory of the firm.
But whereas the traditional emphasis in microeconomics is on the
relationship between profits and the volume of output, with the
amount of capital input taken as fixed, the theory of financial management is expressly concerned with the relationship between
profitability and the volume of capital used.

Financial management is also an extension of prior work in
capital theory. However, the bulk of traditional work in this field
abstracts from the problem of uncertainty and bypasses the problem created by the existence of different types of capital funds.
In contrast, the theory of financial management is specifically
interested in the phenomenon of many types of capital funds and in
the interaction between the mix of financing and the evaluation of
uncertain investments.

Both these extensions are in the direction of a lower degree
of abstraction and toward a more explicit treatment of variables
found in the real world. The theory of financial management is
also an extension of the subject matter contained in the traditional

field of corporation finance and financial institutions, but this extension is in the opposite direction to those noted above. Traditional work in corporation finance and financial institutions is concerned with the relationship between an enterprise and its sources of financing but the emphasis is on specific procedural details of this relationship. The theory of financial management abstracts from some of this realism in order to isolate and identify the broad economic relationships involved and their implications for the formulation of rational business policies aimed at the optimal use, procurement, and allocation of capital funds.

NOTES

1. For two useful discussions of organizational practices in the field of finance, see Weston, "The Finance Function," The Journal of Finance IX, 265-82, and Voorhies, "The Treasurer and the Controller," in Doris, ed., Corporate Treasurer's and Controller's Handbook, pp. 1-50.

2. Harris, "The Financial Executive's Part in Management," Financial Executives' Series: No. 1.

3. An exception is McKinsey and Meech, Controlling the Finances of a Business.

4. Arthur S. Dewing, The Financial Policy of Corporations (New York, Ronald Press, 1920; successive editions: 1926, 1934, 1941.)

5. The best evidence of dissatisfaction with the content of traditional work is to be found in the prefaces of the very large number of texts and editions of texts published during the past forty years. While the actual content of most of these mirrors the traditional pattern of treatment, their prefaces invariably refer to the need for change in scope, emphasis, or treatment.

6. For a constructive suggestion, see Pearson Hunt's review of the 1941 edition of Dewing's book "The Financial Policy of Corporations," Quarterly Journal of Economics, LVIII, 303-13. Recent discussions on these and similar issues may be found in Upton, "Conference on the Teaching of Business Finance," The Journal of Finance, IV, 243; F.J. Calkins, Pearson Hunt, Chelcie C. Bosland, and R. Miller Upton, "Materials and Methods of Teaching Business Finance," The Journal of Finance, V (September, 1950), 270-92; Dauten, et al., "Toward a Theory of Business Finance," The Journal of Finance, X, 107-43.

7. Gordon and Howell, Higher Education for Business; Pierson, The Education of American Businessmen.

8. See, for example, Jack Hirshleifer, James D. DeHaven, and Jerome

W. Milliman, Water Supply: <u>Economics, Technology and Policy</u>, RAND
Corporation Research Study (University of Chicago Press, 1960).

   9. See, for example, Gregory Grossman, ed., <u>Value and Plan</u> (Berkeley, University of California Press, 1960).

   10. Robbins and Foster, Jr., "Profit-Planning and the Finance Function," <u>The Journal of Finance</u>, XII, 451-67.

   11. See Weston, "The Finance Function," <u>The Journal of Finance</u>,
IX, 265-82.

II. THE OBJECTIVE OF FINANCIAL MANAGEMENT

Theory, in a normative sense, is concerned with establishing a mental scheme of things to be done and appropriate ways of doing them. The preceding chapter outlined the major decisions confronting financial management: the amount and composition of investment in assets and the volume and structure of financing. The rest of this book analyzes the problem of how these decisions should be made. But rational decisions presuppose well-defined goals and before we can proceed with our analysis it is necessary first to agree upon the objectives toward which financial decisions should be directed.

The over-all business objective which has been put forward most frequently for purposes of theoretical analysis is that of profit-maximization. This is the goal which is still assumed within the main corpus of economics.[1] However the appropriateness of profit-maximization as a goal has been under increasing attack during the past thirty years and the volume of dissent is now very large.

The earlier challenges to profit-maximization were essentially indictments of the private enterprise system as a whole and were concerned largely with its workability or fairness. The more recent dissent comes from those who basically accept the private enterprise system but who reject profit-maximization because they believe either that it should not be the goal or that it is not the goal of business or that it is not the objective businessmen say they pursue.

The changing attitude toward profit-maximization can be traced to changes in the structure of business itself. In its original form the concept of profit-maximization was simply the logical extension of the legal concept of a business entity within a system based on private property rights and freedom of enterprise. In such a system business represents the free exercise of an owner's right to dispose of his property as he sees fit. It was expected and assumed that owners would see fit to employ their property for their own maximum profit. In this view the function of management, if it does not coincide with ownership, is to serve as trustee for the owners and to obtain maximum long-run profits on their behalf.

When the economic theory of a competitive free enterprise system was formulated, a second and stronger rationale for profit-maximization developed. This is that the individual search for maximum profit provides the "invisible hand" by which social economic welfare is also maximized. In this view the businessman "by directing...industry in such a manner as its produce may be of the greatest value...intends only his own gain, and he is in this, as in many other cases, led by an invisible hand to promote an end which was not part of this intention. Nor is it always the worse for the society that it was no part of it. By pursuing his own interest he frequently promotes that of the society more effectually than when he really intends to promote it. I have never known much good done by those who affected to trade for the public good. It is an affectation, indeed, not very common among merchants."[2]

Today the "affectation," as Smith called it, is very common indeed and it is in fact an integral part of the newer managerial ideology. In this ideology, the owner-manager of the classical system, interested solely in his own gain, has been replaced by the professional manager who serves as trustee, not only for owners but for all parties connected with the enterprise, including employees, customers, suppliers, creditors, the government, the general public, and management itself. In this newer ideology, profit-maximization is regarded as unrealistic, difficult, inappropriate, and immoral.[3] In its place we have a constellation of objectives including service, survival, sales, personal satisfaction, and satisfactory profits. Businessmen who occasionally lapse into talk about profit-maximization are chastised for it. For example: "It is surprising and ironical, that, to judge by what businessmen often say, one would think that they, too, agree that the nature of business corporations is exactly and precisely what critics say it is; namely, that the corporation has no other purpose and recognizes no other criterion of decisions except profits, and that it pursues these profits, just as singlemindedly and irresponsibly as it can."[4]

Apart from a uniform objection to the goal of profit-maximization, the modern commentary on over-all business objectives contains a wide difference of opinion about what these objectives actually are, or should be, or are said to be. Hence it does not provide us with an operationally useful goal on which an entire theory of business management can be based. Fortunately for our present purpose we do not need a total objective which encompasses all business decisions. All we do need is an explicit objective for financial decisions on internal investment and its financing, and this can be defined even if the broader issue of what the total objective of business should be remains unsettled.[5] In short we can sidestep the broader question and confine ourselves to the task of developing a workable definition of the narrower criterion by which to judge a specific set of business decisions.

Profitability vs. Profits

It is useful to distinguish between profits and profitability. The first is an owner-oriented concept. It refers to the amount and share of the national income which goes to those who provide the equity capital for business enterprise. It is concerned with the creation of maximum wealth for owners and the simultaneous distribution of this wealth to them or to their account within the enterprise.

The second is an operational concept, concerned only with the production or creation of new wealth. In this more restricted sense the potential profitability of different courses of action provides the criterion for economizing the use of social resources, and profit-maximization is simply the quest for economic efficiency. It may, but need not contain any inference whatever about what is done with the benefits which an individual firm derives from its more efficient usage of resources, or about how the potential increase in income and wealth to which it leads should be shared.

Maximization of profit in the first sense is what gives rise to most of the present controversy and to much of the dissent that has been expressed. The concept that a business has no other purpose or recognizes no other basis for action than to maximize the amount of wealth accruing to stockholders is clearly unrealistic, and many of the arguments raised against this concept are probably justified.

If we look only at the second sense in which it can be understood, most of these objections to profit-maximization evaporate. Profitability exists when there is the possibility of using resources to yield higher economic values than the joint values of the inputs required. Profitability as a guide to action and profit-maximization in this sense is simply the selection of those assets, projects, and decisions which are profitable and the rejection of those which are not. The purpose of the guide is to ensure the use of the optimum volume and combination of resources in order to maximize the creation of economic value by an enterprise. Most of these processes involve financial decisions and hence profit-maximization in this sense is an appropriate objective for financial management.

Business management is concerned with a much broader sphere of activity and a wider range of decisions. The most obvious of these is what to do with the values created through the investment and financing decisions which are geared to the objective of profit-maximization. These values can be given to customers, to employees (directly or indirectly), to charity, to management itself, or to owners. It is entirely possible, for example, for management to decide what owners will be given only enough to compensate them fairly for the use of their capital in investments that offer less than completely certain returns, with any excess being given to other groups with which the enterprise is connected. Thus it is perfectly legitimate for an enterprise to have profit-maximization in the narrow sense as the ruling objective for investment decisions, but at the same time to aim only at a "satisfactory" level of profits for owners. By the same token, it would also be perfectly rational for the individual plant or firm in a totally socialist economy to use profit-maximization as a guiding objective for decisions.

However, profit-maximization is a phrase which can easily lead to semantic muddles and it is probably hazardous to use it in the special and restricted sense of an operational objective. Happily, for technical reasons, profit-maximization even in this narrow sense turns out to be an unsuitable concept for the operating objective we are seeking. We can therefore drop it and the confusion to which its use inevitably leads.

Profit-Maximization vs. Wealth-Maximization

The technical objection to profit-maximization as an operational criterion for wealth-creating decisions is that it does not provide an operationally feasible measure for ranking alternative courses of action in terms of their economic efficiency, except under very limited assumptions. It suffers from three flaws:

1. It is vague. Like most shorthand expressions it is conveniently brief and familiar but inconveniently loose and hence a source of ambiguity. Which particular definition of profits should be maximized, short-run or long-run? the rate of profit or the amount? profits in the sense of total returns to capital? total returns to stockholders? returns to common shareholders only? profits over and above some allowance for the coverage of normal interest and wages on the owners' capital and time? profits which will be reported by the conventional accounting process or profits adjusted to take account of factors which lie outside the purview of this process? Most of these ambiguities can be resolved by defining profitability more precisely, but it is preferable to use a more precise phrase rather than one which already has different meanings for different people.

2. A more important objection to profit-maximization as a criterion is that it cannot help us to decide between two courses of action which offer benefits that differ with respect to their timing. One apparent solution in such cases is to convert the expected benefit streams into a rate of profit per annum, but as we shall see, these rates do not necessarily rank alternative courses of action in terms of their desirability.

3. The third and most important objection is that the profit-maximization criterion ignores the quality of the expected benefits. In an uncertain world neither the amount nor the rate of profitability provide a basis for selection. In addition we must take into account the quality of benefits, where quality refers to the degree of certainty with which the benefits can be expected. In order to do this we need a single measure which combines both the quantity and the quality dimensions of benefits expected from each course of financial action. Such a measure would be a superior basis for guiding decisions and hence provides a superior basis for stating the operating objective of financial management.

One solution to the problem of the quality and timing of benefits is to think in terms of the utility of expected benefits rather than their amount or rate, where utility reflects the subjective preference for one set of outcomes as against another. But this raises more questions than it answers. Whose utility scales do we use—the owners', management's, or society's? And how do we measure utility preferences so that this criterion can lead to decisions? The approach does not provide a solution to these difficulties. To use an analogy, the utility approach takes the swimmer some distance from the shore and leaves him there, out of his depth.

An alternative and useful solution is provided by the concept of wealth-maximization or net present worth maximization.

The gross present worth of a course of action is equal to the capitalized value of the flow of future expected benefits, discounted (or capitalized) at a rate which reflects their certainty or uncertainty. Wealth or net present worth is the difference between gross present worth and the amount of capital investment required to achieve the benefits being discussed. Any financial action which creates wealth or which has a net present worth above zero is a desirable one and should be undertaken. Any financial action which does not meet this test should be rejected. If two or more desirable courses of action are mutually exclusive (i.e., if only one can be undertaken), then the decision should be to do that which creates most wealth or shows the greatest amount of net present worth. In short, the operating objective for financial management is to maximize wealth or net present worth.

Net Present Worth

In order to define the net present worth of an asset or a course of action more exactly, it is useful to begin by thinking in terms of benefits that are not expected to undergo secular growth or decay. In this case we can define net present worth precisely as follows:

Let G be the average future flow of gross annual earnings expected from an asset or a course of action, before any allowance for depreciation or depletion and before taxes, interest and other prior charges are deducted.[6]

Let M be the average annual reinvestment required to maintain G at the projected level. M may be larger or smaller than the conventionally allowed deductions for depreciation and depletion.

Let T be the expected annual outflow on account of taxes payable, conventionally computed on the basis of taxable property and the flow of income consonant with a gross flow of G.

Let I be the expected flow of annual payments on account of interest, preferred dividends and other prior charges to external sources of nonowner capital.

Then the expected flow of all future net returns attributable to the asset can be defined as a perpetual stream equal to E per annum, where $E = G - (M + I + T)$. For the simple case, in which E contains no growth trend, it is clear that the expected flow of annual dividends to owners, D, is also equal to $G - (M + I + T)$.

Let the rate k measure the degree of uncertainty attaching to the estimates underlying the expected flow of benefits E.

Like E, the rate k is a subjective estimate made by management, and like E it is a subjective estimate which is tied closely to objective values which can be measured in the marketplace, i.e., it is a rate which reflects the aggregate opinion of the market as a whole.

For our simple case of constant average returns, the gross present worth of the asset in question is given by: $V = E/k$. It should be noted that in this formula k, the discount rate or capitalization used as a measure of the quality of E, is expressed in decimal notation rather than in the conventional percentage terminology. Thus, for example, a discount rate of 20 percent per annum would be written as $k = .20$.[7]

Wealth or net present worth W is equal to gross present worth minus the amount of equity capital C required to acquire the asset or to pursue the course of action under consideration. In symbols: $W = V - C$.

W is a compound number which reflects the size of future benefits, E, their quality k and C the amount of capital input required to achieve these benefits.

All this is entirely conceptual. The difficult part of the task is to measure E, and it is probably even more difficult to set k. However, the conceptual formula is also an essential component of the analysis involved in the decision process. Its function is to tell us what should be measured and how these measures should be combined in order to yield a correct decision. The maximization of net present worth is a more complete, and hence a better formulation of the goal, than the maximization of E.

In addition to the explicit inclusion of the quality dimension of E, the net present worth formulation can also handle problems associated with the time dimension of E. Thus far we have confined the discussion to the simple case where E is a steady perpetual flow without any growth trend. In this special case the problem of the time dimension of its components does not arise. But there are many situations in which management must choose between two or more streams of E which differ not only in total size or quality but in timing as well. The simple maximization of E cannot handle such situations unambiguously or correctly. The net present worth formulation can. Hence it provides an unambiguous measure of what financial management should seek to maximize in making investment and financing decisions.

The Rationale for Wealth-Maximization

The basic rationale for the objective of wealth-maximization, in the sense described above, is that it reflects the most efficient use of society's economic resources and thus leads to a maximization of society's economic wealth. However it is useful to explore the implications of this objective of financial management from the various viewpoints involved—of owners, of management, and of society as a whole.

The Owner Point of View. Maximizing W as an operating objective for financial decisions is compatible with a whole range of goals which a company may have with respect to the economic welfare of owners. At one extreme, an enterprise may wish to conform to the classical view that owners or their appointed managers should try to maximize the wealth of owners. Maximizing W is quite compatible with this goal. Indeed, it is essential to it.

At the other extreme we may have a state-owned business enterprise where owners as such do not exist. Maximizing W is also a defensible objective for investment and financial decisions for such an enterprise, because society benefits if this operating objective is pursued.[8]

Between the classical and the anticlassical extremes we have the intermediate case in which business policy aims at some "satisfactory" level of rewards for owners. Whatever policies top management may adopt with regard to the use of business funds for nonowners, the owners are always better off if investment and financial decisions seek to maximize W than if some

alternative objective for decisions is used. The chances of owners getting the satisfactory level of rewards is higher when W is
higher. So are their chances of getting any rewards above the
satisfactory level. In either case maximizing W serves the owners' interests better than any other alternative.

In general, for any existing policy a company may have with
respect to product-pricing, working conditions, wages, and char-
itable contributions, any change in net present worth W will bring
about corresponding change in the wealth of owners. Thus, other
things being equal, the maximization of W is a necessary condition for the maximization of owners' wealth.

Society's Point of View. The use of wealth-maximization as an
operating objective for business investment and financial policy
also maximizes the value of economic output available from a
given level of input, measured at prices prevailing in the market.
Thus it is a necessary condition for maximizing economic welfare
for society as a whole. The argument is similar to that which un-
derlies the "invisible hand" in the classical economic system. It
is also subject to some of the same basic limitations, namely, that
while it is a necessary condition, it may not be a sufficient condition for maximizing economic welfare. But this is a question for
social economic policy rather than for company economic policy.
For example there may be many sectors, such as education or
highways, about which there is general agreement that the wealth
maximization criterion for investment does not lead to socially
optimal decisions. In these cases, the sectors require public
rather than private investment. Similarly, it can be argued that
the resources which are economized by private financial decisions
may become unemployed rather than released for alternative productive uses and that , as a consequence, total social wealth may
not be increased. But again, this is a matter for public rather
than company policy. Finally, and this can be an important issue
in those economies which control wages and prices, the prices
used in evaluating investment and financial decisions may not reflect true values. In this situation the wealth-maximization objective may lead to decisions which are wrong from the point of
view of society's true interests. But here too the fault is not with
the wealth-maximization criterion, but rather with the errors
being made by those who control the framework in which the individual enterprise makes decisions.[9]

If the over-all social and economic policy is an enlightened one, wealth-maximization by each individual enterprise will also maximize social-economic welfare. If the social-economic framework is unenlightened or wrong, maximum economic welfare cannot be achieved, but the highest attainable level which can be consistently achieved is that associated with an individual company policy based on maximizing W.

Management's Point of View. It is harder to reconcile the operating objective of maximizing W with management's point of view. Unlike the owner viewpoint or the social viewpoint, the management viewpoint cannot easily be summarized in terms of some simple maximum.

Some managements may be interested in maximum performance as measured by the wealth they succeed in creating for owners, or by the net present worth they are able to create for society as a whole. In either case the coincidence of interests between management's viewpoint and the wealth-maximization criterion is clear and simple.

But what if management has other motives, such as maximizing sales or size, growth or market share, or their own survival, or peace of mind? These operating goals do not necessarily conflict with the operating goal of wealth-maximization. Indeed, a good case could be made for the thesis that wealth-maximization also maximizes the achievement of these other objectives. But the point of issue is what if there is a conflict? What, for example, if management's quest for its own peace of mind or for some other goal consistently leads it to reject operating decisions that should be accepted by the wealth-maximizing criterion?

The traditional answer is that such a management will be replaced sooner or later, and this is the only answer possible. Legally, management governs only as the appointed representatives of the owners. It may reject over-all goals which promote the exclusive interest of owners so long as it substitutes goals which are designed to promote that of society as a whole. But if it rejects owner-oriented goals and socially-oriented goals in favor of goals that are solely management-oriented and which lead to substantially different courses of action, its right to govern is open to question.

As far as resource-using decisions are concerned the criterion of wealth-maximization provides a meaningful objective which effectively promotes the long-run welfare of society as well as that of the owners of a business enterprise. We will therefore adopt the maximization of wealth, or net present wealth, as the operating objective by which financial decisions should be guided.

NOTES

1. For a quick survey of this assumption in economic texts, see Anthony, "The Trouble with Profit-Maximization," Harvard Business Review, XXXVIII, 126-34.

2. Adam Smith, The Wealth of Nations, Cannan Edition (New York, The Modern Library, 1937), p. 423.

3. See Anthony, "The Trouble with Profit-Maximization," Harvard Business Review, XXXVIII, 126-34.

4. Glover, The Attack on Big Business, p. 328.

5. For recent discussions of the broader issues, see Sutton, Harris, Kaysen, and Tobin, The American Business Creed: Margolis, "The Analysis of the Firm: Rationalism, Conventionalism and Behaviorism," Journal of Business, XX, 187-89; March and Simon, Organizations; Mason, "The Apologetics of Managerialism," Journal of Business, XXXI, 1-11; and Glover, The Attack on Big Business.

6. The use of the term "expected earnings" (or dividends or reinvestments or taxes) in this section and throughout the book does not imply that these are simple single-valued anticipations. What is expected is generally a whole range of outcomes with a different probability attaching to each. "Expected value" is simply a shorthand and commonsense way of expressing the mathematical expectation of the subjective probability distribution of the range of outcomes anticipated by those making the estimate.

7. The proof that $V = E/k$ can be derived from the summation of a geometric progression is as follows:

Let $E_1, E_3 \ldots E_\infty$ be the flow of E expected in years 1, 2, 3, ... ∞

Then

$$V = \frac{E_1}{1 + k} + \frac{E_2}{(1 + k)^2} + \cdots \frac{E}{(1 + k)^\infty}$$

$$= E \cdot \left[\frac{1}{1 + k} + \left(\frac{1}{1 + k}\right)^2 + \cdots \left(\frac{1}{1 + k}\right)^\infty \right]$$

$$= E \cdot \frac{1}{1 + k} \left[1 + \left(\frac{1}{1 + k}\right)^2 + \cdots \left(\frac{1}{1 + k}\right)^\infty \right].$$

Putting $(1/1 + k) = r$, the sum of geometric progression within the square brackets is given by the formula $1/1 - r$.

This is equal to

$$\frac{1}{1 - \left(\dfrac{1}{1+k}\right)} \text{ or } \frac{1+k}{k}$$

Thus

$$V = E \cdot \frac{1}{1+k} \cdot \frac{1+k}{k} = \frac{E}{k}$$

For benefit streams in which E_1, E_2, E_3, k are not equal, the value of V cannot be simplified beyond the statement in equation 2.1.

8. For various accounts of the increasing awareness of profitability as a criterion for resource-allocation decisions behind the Iron Curtain, see Grossman, ed., Value and Plan (Berkeley, University of California Press, 1960).

9. It is possible to think of an analogous problem within a large company operating in a free-enterprise framework. If the prices of internal transfers between divisions of such a company are set incorrectly by top management policy, it is possible that the individual profit centers may pursue policies that maximize their own showing but do not maximize W for the company as a whole.

III. THE CONCEPT OF THE COST OF CAPITAL

The decision process implied by the goal of maximizing net present worth can be stated in operational terms in two ways. Any business proposal requiring the use of funds can be expected to increase net present worth and hence should be accepted:

1. If the present worth of the estimated stream of net incremental benefits it promises is larger than the present worth of the estimated stream of net capital outlays required for its implementation, when both streams are capitalized (or discounted) at a rate k that measures the "cost of capital."

2. If the rate of return it promises (correctly computed from expected outlays and benefits) exceeds the cost of capital k.

These two formulations yield identical answers as far as accept or reject investment decisions are concerned. This is so because the present worth of benefits will exceed the present worth of outlays if, and only if, the rate of return exceeds the cost of capital.

Both these approaches will identify all available proposals that promise to increase net present worth.[1] Both require acceptable estimates of net outlays and net incremental benefits. Finally, both depend heavily on a correct measure of k, the cost of capital. This serves in either formulation as a fundamental standard of financial performance that determines the acceptability of all uses of funds.

What is k and how should it be measured? This is clearly the central question facing financial management. The definition of k as the cost of capital is only one way of expressing its nature and function and perhaps it is not the most useful way. Other descriptions of its role exist. Thus k has been referred to as (a) the minimum required rate of return on proposals using capital funds, (b) the cutoff rate for capital expenditures, (c) the "hurdle" rate or "target" rate of return which must be surpassed if capital-use is to be justified, (d) the financial standard. Together, these describe the function it performs in the process of making correct capital allocation decisions more adequately than does the phrase, cost of capital. But cost of capital is the only description which focuses on the way k is derived and therefore insists that it must be set in accordance with conditions at which the enterprise is able to obtain funds in the capital market for the purpose it has in mind and at the time it wishes to raise the required funds.

Most of the conceptual difficulty in measuring k arises from two factors. One is uncertainty: business funds are generally used for purposes that do not offer definite, sure returns. The second is an institutional outgrowth of the first: business funds can be derived through a huge variety of financial instruments. These range from pure debt, at the one extreme, which requires definite periodic payments that cannot be defaulted on without serious injury to the owners of the enterprise, to pure equity contributions, at the other extreme, which require virtually no contractual commitments except for equitable treatment along with other owners. Between, there is a mix of available instruments involving ownership, creditor, income, and control rights in varying degrees, with possible combinations limited only by the ingenuity of the capital markets and of those who manage the financing problems of an enterprise.

The Special Case of Complete Certainty

In a hypothetical world of complete certainty, k would also be an essential element in a rational capital allocation process designed to maximize net present worth. Setting k in such a world is an easy task. In a world of complete certainty k is simply equal to the rate of interest i, and all proposals offering the definite certainty of a rate of return greater than i would satisfy the criterion of net present worth maximization. Alternatively all proposals that contribute benefits whose present worth (capitalized at the rate i) is larger than the outlay required should be accepted. In such a hypothetical world, the expected return on capital is as certain and definite as the cost of capital which is derived from the source that requires the most definite obligation to repay— namely, pure debt. One can be compared directly with the other without any allowance for differential uncertainties. Nor does the difficult problem of different kinds of capital arise, because in a world of complete certainty there would be little distinction between debt and equity, or among the intermediate variants that exist in a world in which uncertainty prevails.

The solution that $k = i$ in an assumed world of certainty is not immediately helpful when we remove this assumption and face the problem of measuring k for an individual enterprise, in a world in which the investment of funds promises uncertain benefits and in which the funds themselves may be derived in various forms, at varying nominal costs, and with a varying impact on the quantity and quality of the residual earnings that accrue to owners. However, the certainty solution, or the certainty equivalent solution, does provide a valuable point of departure and a number of useful insights.[2]

It takes the first step in extending the basic concept of economic efficiency or profitability to situations that involve time and the use of capital funds. The basic concept itself is that profit is simply the difference between the total cost of production and the market value of the product. Where there is no time interval between production and sale, no capital is involved, and the problem of identifying profitable opportunities is simply a matter of comparing the value of outputs against inputs or revenues against cost. The prescription for action is equally straightforward. Inputs of various types of labor and materials should be increased so long as the incremental value of output attributable to each increased input exceeds the cost of the input.

When we move to situations in which there is a time interval between inputs and the sale of outputs (i.e., between outlays and receipts), the use of capital funds is involved in the business process, and the identification of economic efficiency or profitability is no longer obvious. The general solution is simply an extension of the simpler case described above: profitability exists when revenues exceed costs, including an allowance for the cost of capital funds required. The corresponding prescription for optimal action is that inputs of capital (investment) should continue to be made so long as the incremental benefits attributable to these added inputs exceeds the incremental cost of the capital required. But this general solution does not specify how the cost of capital is measured or how exactly this measure should be incorporated into the analysis.

The hypothetical case of complete certainty does provide an answer to the second of these problems. In this case, the relevant measure for the cost of capital is the market rate of interest and the analysis of profitability can be conducted in either of two ways:

1. The rate of interest can be used to adjust the values of expected outlays and receipts, which take place over time, to a single reference point of time. The reference point generally used is the present, i.e., we measure the present value of expected receipts and outlays. Profitability exists when the present value of receipts expected from an increment of investment exceeds the present value of outlays required to implement the investment.

2. Alternatively, the anticipated benefits can be expressed as a rate of return relative to the outlays required to achieve them. This gives a single measure of gross profitability, which is expressed as a rate per annum and which takes into account the volume as well as the timing of anticipated outlays and revenues, but which does not take into account the cost of capital. Net profitability exists when a proposal offers a rate of return larger than the rate of interest.

This highly condensed version of investment analysis under conditions of certainty[3] focuses on the basic function performed by the cost of capital, namely that it measures the cost of capital inputs. Like any other cost the cost of capital is a hurdle or a minimum which must be exceeded by incremental revenues attributable to its use, if its use is to be justified.

However there are two related functions which the cost of capital performs. A firm which is faced with a number of investment proposals or opportunities to use capital will presumably want to accept them in descending order of profitability. In order to do this it must first rank the proposals in this order. The cost of capital is an important element in the ranking process and in the associated process of selecting the better of two competing alternatives.[4] Second, from the point of view of the capital allocation budget as a whole, the cost of capital provides an objective cutoff point for appropriations. Proposals offering rewards higher than this point are accepted, those not offering such rewards are rejected.

The hypothetical case of complete certainty provides a useful description of the role of the cost of capital as a financial criterion for accepting a capital-using proposal, as an integral part of the selection of mechanism which chooses between two or more competitive ways of doing something, and as a cutoff point for determining total capital expenditures.

The certainty-model also provides additional insights. One of these is that true profitability, or economic efficiency, is not an absolute attribute, but depends intimately on prevailing market rates of interest. Thus a proposal that is economically efficient and hence desirable in one economy or at one point of time may not be so in another economy or at another time, if the cost of capital is different. Similarly, two alternative techniques of production may rank one way in one economy and in an opposite way in a second economy, again depending on differences in the prevailing cost of capital in the two areas.

The Problem of Uncertainty

If we lift the artificial assumption of completely certain or certainty-equivalent returns from investment in assets, the rate of interest is no longer an appropriate measure of the cost of capital.

In the real world the returns promised by a proposal can be estimated and expressed quantitatively but the estimates themselves are subject to unmeasurable degrees of uncertainty. Profitability cannot be identified by comparing these indefinite expectations of return against the rate of interest paid on borrowed funds.

First, some substantial part of the financing for company investment is provided by owners in the form of equity capital. The rate of interest is not a relevant measure of the cost of these funds. Second, there is nothing indefinite or uncertain about the company's liability for interest payments on borrowed funds it does use. These liabilities are contractual and definite, and the rate of interest charged on debt contracts reflects this fact. In contrast, the rate of return promised by an investment proposal is at best an uncertain estimate of the future. Hence the acceptability of a proposal cannot be ascertained by a simple comparison between these two rates.

What we want is a basis for measuring a company's cost of capital under realistic conditions of economic and political uncertainty. Such a measure is needed for the same purposes as those provided by the rate of interest in an artificial world of

complete certainty, namely, as a financial standard against which
relative profitability can be screened, as a minimum acceptable
rate of return, and as a defensible basis for setting a cutoff point
for capital expenditures.

A realistic measure of k must take into account the general
uncertainty of future returns on present capital investment and
the fact that different uses of funds within the same company may
involve different degrees of uncertainty. It must also take into
account the fact that capital funds can be derived in many different ways and that each combination of financing available has a
different effect on the quantity and quality of the net residual
benefits which will accrue to owners of the enterprise. Finally,
like the rate of interest in the certainty-model, the measure of
cost of capital must reflect changing conditions in the capital
markets from which all funds are ultimately derived.

A frontal attack on the problem of measuring the cost of capital in operational terms is a recent phenomenon. Prior to this
development the problem was either ignored or bypassed. The
focus of traditional economic theory was on refinements to the
certainty or certainty-equivalent models of investment analysis.
Traditional work in corporate financial policy has been far less
abstract, but the vast commentary developed around questions of
corporate expansion and growth provides no explicit discussion
of the central issues.

Business itself has not been able to sidestep the task of setting
financial standards in an uncertain world. Presumably management has always had to set minimum standards of required performance and to decide the size and composition of capital expenditures. Whether or not these standards were expressed in terms of
"the cost of capital"—which is still largely an academic term—management has had to develop some basis for making these decisions.

What are the bases used by business and how were they derived? Unfortunately we have little useful documentation on this
subject, and explicit documentation is difficult to obtain. There
is the usual difficulty caused by the fact that the actual conduct
of business decisions may not be adequately reflected by what
business spokesmen say they do. In addition, decisions on investment and growth are such broad ones it is easy and indeed
irresistible to argue that they are made on the basis of a whole
constellation of variables, and this of course evades the questions
of how specific minimum standards of financial performance are

set or what they are. Finally, "high finance" has traditionally been conducted in a citadel, close to the top, and the top has always been reticent about stating its own logic explicitly.

So far as we know, business has developed a variety of approaches to guide the basic investment decisions which theory now suggests should be guided by an explicit measure of the cost of capital. These approaches range from rules-of-thumb to fairly well-crystallized "theories."

One common approach is first to set the total volume of capital expansion on the basis of broad financial policy and then to allocate this preset amount among competing uses. A revered recipe for setting the cutoff point for the amount of expenditures is the New England Theory of business expansion, which limits the amount of capital expansion in any period to the volume of profits being earned in that period. An alternative approach for determining the volume of expenditures is to spend enough to maintain a company's relative position in a growing economy.

Apparently these and similar approaches pay no explicit attention to the volume or profitability of new investment opportunities available or to the cost and other conditions under which internal capital can be raised. Many firms have prospered using these recipes but it is hard to believe that they would not have done even better without them.

An alternative rule of action as revered as the New England Theory is that provided by the Banker Theory of business expansion. In one of the standard works in the field, the rule is interpreted as follows: "This theory amounts to the proposition that expansion by borrowing should occur when, as and if the rate of earnings on the added capital is in excess of the rate paid by the corporation for that capital." [5]

Undaunted by the conflict between the two prescriptions the author argues: "In so far as it is possible to deduce general rules with respect to the utilization of these two theories, the following appear sound: (1) Industries with a large proportion of fixed capital should employ the New England Theory. (2) Industries with a large percentage of liquid assets lean toward the Banker Theory." [6]

These theories and recipes are not put forward today as widely or as explicitly as they were twenty-five years ago. Instead, more and more enterprises appear to have a formal or informal standard of minimum financial performance in mind, against which the profitability of investment opportunities are assayed. Sometimes these standards take the form of a minimum payoff period within which capital-using proposals must return the funds invested in them. The use of a payoff period as an investment criterion implies some minimum rate of return, but since the implied rate depends not only on the length of the payoff period required but also on the expected useful life of the asset, the rate implied by any given payoff period is hard to measure.

In some companies the minimum required rates or target rates are set quite explicitly for the purpose of guiding pricing and investment decisions. While the precise bases on which these rates are set are rarely announced they do provide useful measures of what management in various industries feels a fair rate ought to be. The most complete evidence for this is contained in a recent study of pricing objectives in large companies.[7] The companies in this study which employed target rates of return of investment and the rates used are listed below:

Company	Target Rate on Investment
Alcoa	20 percent (after taxes); higher on new products
Du Pont	No specific figure given
Esso (Standard Oil of N. J.)	"Fair return"—no specific figure given
General Electric	20 percent (after taxes)
General Motors	20 percent (after taxes)
International Harvester	10 percent (after taxes)
Johns-Manville	Return on investment greater than last 15-year average (about 15 percent after taxes); higher target for new products
Kroger	(Collateral goal); target return of 20 percent (before taxes)
Standard Oil (Indiana)	Target return on investment (none specified)
Sears Roebuck	(Collateral goal); realization of traditional return on investment of 10-15 percent (after taxes)
Union Carbide	Target return on investment[a]
U. S. Steel	8 percent (after taxes)

Source: Lanzilotti, "Pricing Objectives in Large Companies," American Economic Review, XLVIII, 921-40.
[a] In discussion with management officials various profit returns were mentioned, with considerable variation among divisions of the company. No official profit target percentage was given, but the author estimates the average profit objective for the corporation to be approximately 35 percent before taxes or an effective rate after taxes of about 18 percent.

Presumably these target rates perform some of the functions we have ascribed to the cost of capital and presumably there is a growing interest in setting these rates explicitly. We turn now to the analytical question of how this should be done.

If the purpose of a target or minimum rate is simply to prevent unwise investment decisions, i.e., those which reduce net present worth, it is easy to set the rate high enough to avoid such sins of commission. But its purpose is also to ensure that investment proposals which can be expected to increase net present worth are not rejected. This requires a more exact basis for setting screening standards, and for altering them in the light of changes in the capital markets and variations in the quality of returns expected from the investment or reinvestment of funds. The problem is a complex one and it is useful to conduct the analysis in stages. To begin, we will assume that all proposed uses of funds by a given enterprise promise returns which are of like quality, as far as degree of certainty or uncertainty is concerned, as those expected from existing investments. Later in the analysis we will lift this assumption.

Within the assumption of homogeneous returns (homogeneous with respect to quality) it is convenient to proceed in two broad steps, first dealing with the question of the cost of capital for companies which finance exclusively with pure equity funds and later taking up the question of measuring the cost of capital derived from a combination of debt and equity financing.

NOTES

1. Strictly speaking, it is necessary to assume that no proposal under consideration ever displaces a superior use of funds. The problem of choosing the best of two or more mutually exclusive proposals is discussed more completely in a later chapter.

2. The certainty-equivalent situation is one in which expected returns are not definite but may vary according to a probability distribution which is known. In this case it is simple to convert the probability value of all expected outcomes into a single expected value known as its certainty equivalent. True uncertainty exists when we do not know or cannot apply the probability distribution of expected benefits. For the classic treatment of this matter see Frank H. Knight, Risk, Uncertainty and Profit (Boston and New York, Houghton Mifflin Company, 1921).

3. For a complete discussion of investment criteria under conditions of certainty see Lutz and Lutz, The Theory of Investment of the Firm.

4. Some complex problems involved in the relative ranking of proposals are discussed in a later chapter.

5. Floyd F. Burtchett, Corporation Finance (New York, Harper and Brothers, 1934), p. 730.

6. Burtchett, Corporation Finance, p. 730.

7. Lanzillotti, "Pricing Objectives in Large Companies," American Economic Review, XLVIII, 921-40.

IV. THE COST OF EXTERNAL EQUITY CAPITAL

The use of equity capital does not involve any cost in an accounting sense, except of course for items such as the expense of floating new issues. However, we are interested in the cost of equity in a broader sense. Specifically, we want a correct basis for setting the minimum rate of return required to justify the use of equity funds, correct in that it can always be expected to lead to that set of investment decisions which will maximize net present worth.

The problem is complicated by the fact that equity funds can be derived in more than one way—internally, through gross earnings which are set aside in the form of depreciation and other capital-consumption allowances or by retaining earnings, or externally, through the sale of new issues of common stock directly, through preemptive rights to existing owners, or through conversion privileges granted to other classes of securities.[1] Whatever the form, an investment decision financed by equity sources requires a comparison of returns against the cost of capital, and our problem is how these capital costs should be set in the first place.

This does not imply that a decision to invest equity funds depends solely on the relationship between expected returns and the cost of capital. Other considerations exist, such as management's willingness to expand, the legality of raising equity funds internally or externally, and the question of how control might be affected. But in discussing these considerations it is possible to digress so deeply into the intricacies of psychology and the laws of fifty different states that one does not return to the economic issue itself! We will therefore assume that all other necessary conditions for expansion through equity funds are met in order to concentrate on the basic question: what is the cost of equity capital in the sense of a minimum rate of return that must be surpassed if the investment of funds is to be justified? And we will begin with the simplest case in which the capital required must be derived from a new issue of common stock.

The Cost of Equity from New Issues

Let us begin with a simple numerical example. A company is considering a specific proposal requiring an outlay of $6,000,000 which promises to yield a rate of return of 15 percent per annum, having the same quality as the flow of earnings expected from existing operations. Our hypothetical company has no debt whatever and the funds required for the outlay must be derived from a new issue of common stock. Other data for the company are as follows:[2]

1. Total book value of company (B)	$30,000,000
2. Capitalization	1,000,000 shares
3. Current annual earnings; after taxes (E)	$3,000,000
4. Best estimate of future annual earnings without expansion project (E_A)	$3,300,000
5. Current annual dividend (D)	$2,000,000
6. Best estimate of future annual earnings if expansion project is accepted (E_A)	$4,200,000
7. Current market value per share (M)	$22
8. Net proceeds per share of new issue (net market value) (P)	$20

These data are deliberately simplified and the following simplifying assumptions are worth noting:

(a) We assume that estimates of outlays and future earnings have been accepted as the best available and that they take into account all benefits expected from the two alternative courses of action open to the company—to undertake or not to undertake the project.

(b) We assume that the quality or degree of certainty of future expected earnings with the project is identical to the quality of future expected earnings without the project.

(c) We assume that the conventional book earnings shown (after taxes and depreciation) reflect true earnings, i.e., that the rein-

vestment of depreciation allowances is just sufficient to maintain
the earning rate which is projected. The assumption of a flat trend
for average future earnings greatly simplifies the arithmetic of
the argument. However, it does conflict with the assumption that
about one-third of a company's earnings are being reinvested, and
thus raises the question of why these reinvestments do not add to
future earnings. We will ignore this problem temporarily and
take it up later when we discuss the problem of earnings streams
with growth trends.

(d) We assume that the total issue of new stock is sold to the
public through an investment banker who offers the firm definite
net proceeds of $20 a share.

Given these conditions, we can turn our attention to several
questions: Should the company embark on the proposed project?
Will the project increase the net present worth of existing owners?
In other words, what is the correct basis for setting the minimum
required rate of return against which the promised return of 15
percent on the expansion project must be compared? Or, in more
general terms, how should the cost of equity capital be measured?

There are a number of plausible answers to this question, all
of which have been mentioned both in professional and in academic
literature as relevant criteria for the kind of decision involved in
the problem.

1. Will it dilute book value per share? The argument here is
that the effect of financing on book value is an important consideration. In our example the present book value is $30 per share.
The sale of a new issue at a net price of $20 will clearly dilute
book value. Therefore the investment project should be rejected
if new equity financing is the only available source of funds.

2. What is the effect on "return on investment" (book value
basis)? The argument is that the company has been earning a return of $3 on book investment of $30 per share or a rate of 10
percent. A proposal that offers a rate of return on investment
which is higher than this (but of like quality) is acceptable because
it raises average performance. On this basis, the measure for
the cost of capital would be given by the ratio of current earnings
to present book value, i.e., the ratio E/B or 10 percent in our
example.

A variant of this would look at the effect of the proposal on future return on book investment. In this case, the minimum required rate on new investment must exceed 3.30/30 or 11 percent.

3. Does the promised return exceed dividend requirements?
This criterion implies that the ratio of dividends per share to
net proceeds available per new share issued is the logical basis
for setting the minimum standard of required performance for
new investments. The argument is that a rate of return per share
higher than the dividend requirement per share provides a net
gain to the treasury. The implied measure for the cost of capital
is D/P or 10 percent, in our example.[3]

4. What is the effect on earnings per share? This argues that
the rate of earnings per dollar of net market value is the appropriate measure of the cost of new equity capital. In the present
example this rate is 15 percent if we use the ratio of current
earnings per share to net market value per share. If we use E_A
as the numerator (future expected earnings per share without the
project) the cost of capital would be 16.5 percent.

These points of view provide widely differing answers for the
cost of capital and hence for the investment decision involved. In
any particular case, more than one basis may lead to the right
answer, but one only can be correct as a general basis for setting
the required rate of return so that it always leads to decisions
that can be expected to maximize net present worth.

In our example the only two criteria which would reject the
project are (a) the use of E_A/P as the cost of capital and (b) the
argument that per share book values should never be diluted.
Since acceptance of the proposal can be expected to reduce the
net present worth of the company, the other criteria, which failed
to reject the proposal, cannot provide a generally correct basis
for setting the cost of new equity capital.

The "proof" that acceptance of the project would reduce net
present worth of owners is as follows:

Since net proceeds per share issued is $20, the company must
sell 300,000 shares to finance the outlay of $6,000,000 required
by the proposal. Total earnings with the project are expected to
be $4,200,000 or $3.23 per share for each of the 1,300,000 shares
outstanding after the new issue is floated. But earnings per share
without undertaking the project or the associated new financing
are expected to be $3,300,000 on the 1,000,000 original shares,
or $3.30 per share. Since the quality of expected earnings with
or without the project are assumed to be identical, it must follow
that present owners will suffer a decline in the present worth of
their holdings if the proposal is accepted.

It does not automatically follow that the criteria which wrongly accepted the project are wrong because they always set too low a standard of acceptance. It would be relatively easy to devise a second example in which it can be shown that they err because they set the acceptance too high and therefore reject investment proposals that should be accepted.

Likewise it does not automatically follow that the two criteria which provide a correct decision to reject in our particular example will always provide a correct answer. In fact, we will see shortly that the book value dilution approach is quite untenable as a general criterion for investment action geared to net present worth maximization. However, it can be shown that the use of E_A/P as a measure for the cost of new equity capital does provide a generally correct basis for setting a minimum required rate of earnings, i.e., a basis which will always accept proposals that can be expected to increase net present worth and always reject those that do not.

That E_A/P, or 16.5 percent, in our example, is the correct measure of the minimum earnings rate required on the investment of new funds follows from the function for which this minimum rate is designed. This is to screen proposals according to whether they do or do not increase net present worth. So long as we are assuming that any added earnings have the same quality as earnings from existing investments we can say that the function of the screening standard is to identify proposals that offer to increase earnings per share. Since E_A measures earnings expected from existing investments and since it costs existing owners one share to raise P dollars of new funds, it follows that new investments must generate an earnings rate of at least E_A/P if present owners are to enjoy an increase in earnings per share. The arithmetic of the argument is as follows:

1. Minimum earnings per share required
   if present worth of owners is not to be
   diluted $ 3.30
2. Shares outstanding if project is financed   1,300,000
3. Minimum total earnings required including
   project earnings (item 1 times item 2) $4,290,000
4. Expected earnings without project $3,300,000
5. Minimum earnings to be contributed by
   "acceptable" project (item 3 minus
   item 4) $ 990,000

6. Investment required by project $6,000,000
7. Minimum rate of return required if
   project is to be acceptable (item 5
   divided by item 6)   16.5 percent

   In general, if k_e is the minimum required rate of return on new
equity, S is the number of shares outstanding, and X is the number
of new shares that must be issued, we have:

$$k_e = \frac{E_A(S + X) - E_A(S)}{P \cdot X} = \frac{E_A}{P}$$

   Whether we use E_A/P or k_e, our measure of the minimum required return on new equity is simply the capitalization rate at
which the market values an expected stream of earnings of this
quality.[4] Investment proposals offering a rate of return higher
than k_e but of a quality equal to earnings on existing investment
have a value that is greater than the outlay required to assemble
this value. In other words, these proposals have positive net
present worth and hence they add to the net present worth of the
company. They also increase the net present worth of owners
and raise the market value of shares above what it otherwise
would be. Proposals offering a rate of return less than k_e but of
similar quality to earnings on existing investments have the opposite effect. Stated this way, it is obvious that the logical screening standard for investments financed by new equity funds is given
by the capitalization rate k_e.
   The identification of k_e as the cost of capital and its definition
as the simple ratio of E_A to P applies only to the special case
we have been examining, that of a debt-free company, whose projected earnings contain no trend up or down, which must finance
any proposed investment that it accepts through funds derived by
by a new issue of common stock. This is only the first step in
the analysis and measurement of the cost of capital under realistic conditions. But before we proceed we shall return briefly to
the investment criteria which we have rejected.
   Book Value Dilution. The first criterion we examined rejected
the proposal in our example because it involved a dilution of book
value per share. This criterion provided a correct answer to the
investment decision, but for the wrong reason. Its reason for
rejecting the proposal has nothing to do with the merits of the
investment but is based entirely on the relationship between net

market value per share and net book value. It would reject a proposal that is twice as good as the one under consideration—or, for that matter, one that is a thousand times as good, if its implementation required the sale of new equity securities. On the other hand, if market value per share happens to be higher than book value per share the approach would presumably accept any proposal offering a positive rate of return. Such a criterion is quite untenable as a basis for investment action.

Concern with book value dilution makes sense only under special circumstances. One such circumstance is if merger negotiations or evaluation by a court is expected. In such cases, book value may enter the formula by which value is determined, whether or not a clear-cut market value exists. Because of this fact, and only because of this fact, book value may be important.

A second situation occurs when market values are below book value because of generally depressed conditions in the market for equity shares. In this case the cost of equity capital would also be very high and would therefore provide a high screening standard. But it is possible even under these circumstances to envisage proposals which promise to yield more than the cost-of-capital standard requires. These should be accepted. While alternative forms of financing for the proposals would be better, with subsequent new equity financing timed for a later period when its cost is expected to be lower, the fact remains that an investment opportunity which must be financed with new equity or else completely foregone should be undertaken. In other words, book value dilution per se may influence the form of financing to be used, but it is not the relevant consideration as far as the investment decision is concerned and certainly is not a governing consideration even in the circumstances we are discussing. When the equity market as a whole is not at especially depressed levels, concern with book value dilution can defeat the very objective it aims at, namely, to raise the market value of an individual company's shares to its existing book value. This is so because the only way the objective can be accomplished is through undertaking new investments which offer a higher rate of return (without sacrificing quality) than the capitalization rate at which the market presently values the company. If such investments are vetoed because the financing they require is going to reduce book value per share this will simply ensure that the market will continue to value the company's shares below book value.

Return on Book Investment. In the example discussed earlier, the use of return on book investment as the minimum rate of earnings required on new investment led to the acceptance of a proposal that would have reduced net present worth and hence would have hurt existing stockholders. We therefore rejected this approach to the measurement of the cost of capital. However, return on book investment is a venerable concept in the business world. Unlike the capitalization rate, which relates mere estimates of the future to market prices, the return on book investment has an aura of exactness which it derives from the fact that it is the ratio of two precise numbers which are "correct" to the last dollar, attested to by public accountants, and published widely. Those who are not happy about giving it up too easily are likely to argue that the past return on book investment may not be the only criterion for new investment but that it is one among several criteria, all of which must be met. For this type of argument, the case given in our example proves nothing. It is also necessary to show that book return on investment can be misleading even if it is only one of many criteria that must all be met for a new investment to be accepted.

We can show this simply by changing the value of two items in the example. Let the net market value per share in our example be $40 and book value $15, with all the other facts remaining the same. In this situation the return on book criterion would require a minimum earnings on new investment of 20 percent and the 15 percent proposal would therefore be rejected. Under the new assumptions the minimum acceptance standard k_e would be 8.25 percent (3.30/40), and we would therefore accept the proposal. We can again show that k_e is the basis which provides the right answer, this time because acceptance can be expected to increase per-share earnings and hence the net present worth of owners. In this instance, the return on book criterion is wrong because it rejects an opportunity to create net present worth and to improve the position and wealth of existing stockholders.

A final argument that might be made to salvage the use of past return on book investment as a minimum criterion is that stockholders place a high valuation on the shares (in this case, $40) relative to book value, (in this case, $15) because they believe that the company is willing and able to maintain an earnings rate of 20 percent or so on future investments just as they have on past investments. The implication of this argument is that acceptance of a rate lower than 20 percent would soon disenchant the market, lower the price/earnings ratio at which the shares are valued (i.e., raise the capitalization rate) and hence reduce net present worth and hurt stockholders.

There is no single or clear-cut refutation of this final argument. Market values above net book values are clearly associated with the fact that the rate of earnings is high relative to net book investment. This may be because general prices have risen since the investment was made or because the past use of a book rate of depreciation which is higher than the rate at which the physical or economic life of assets has actually declined since they were acquired. But it does not follow from this that the correct investment policy is to restrict future investments in assets to those offering equally high earnings on current acquisition costs. This point can be seen clearly if we think of a hypothetical company which is earning handsome royalties by leasing land that has virtually no book value because it was acquired long ago. Should this company insist that the only future investments it can accept are those offering an equally high rate of return? The answer is "obviously not."

The argument that market values might suffer if the return-on-net-book standard is not met confuses two rates that should be kept separate—the rate of earnings and the rate at which those earnings are capitalized by the market. The rate at which the market capitalizes future earnings reflects the quality of earnings and is independent of the quantity of these earnings. Given our assumption of homogeneous investments (homogeneous with respect to quality) it is hard to see how investment policy in itself can bring about a change in the capitalization rate at which earnings will be valued.[5]

In other words, the argument that the capitalization rate will be lowered by the acceptance of proposals (of given quality) which yield less than the return being achieved on net book investment is specious.

It is easy to confuse the rate of earnings with the rate at which these earnings are capitalized if one thinks in terms of price-earnings ratios rather than capitalization rates. If market capitalization rates are determined jointly by factors external to the company and by the quality of investments, they will not undergo a change because the investment criterion used is lower than the return on book investment. And if they do not change (for this particular reason) then the correct criterion for new equity investment, i.e., the criterion which will maximize net present worth and hence the long-run market value of shares, is k_e. The fact that return on net book investment is higher than k_e is not relevant to new investment decisions.

The Dividend Rate. The use of the current dividend yield (the ratio of current dividends to net market price) as the measure of cost of capital is misleading on two counts. It is not current dividends (D) but future dividends (D_A) that matter, because this is what present stockholders promise new stockholders when they issue new shares. If the company pays out all its future earnings (E_A) as cash dividends (D_A) it does not matter whether we measure the cost of new equity capital as E_A/P or D_A/P because these are identical measures.

If, however, the company consistently retains part of its earnings for reinvestment we can no longer posit earnings streams or dividend streams with no growth trend. The cost of capital can be correctly formulated either in terms of dividends or of earnings, but because of the growth element it is convenient to defer a discussion of these formulations and to deal with them after the basic concept of growing streams has been explored.

Stock Flotation Through Privileged Subscription

The preceding discussion assumes that the new stock issues are sold to the general public through an investment banker or syndicate. This is not the only method, nor even the most usual method for raising equity funds through a new issue. Issues may be sold by giving existing shareholders a right to subscribe to the new shares at some price below the current market. With this method a variety of arrangements is possible. The stockholder may or may not be given the privilege of transferring to others these rights to buy at a given price; an investment banker's services may or may not be used; if they are used, the cost of these services may differ from the flotation and underwriting expenses involved in a direct sale without the use of rights. Our main interest here is not in the specific mechanics of the sale but in the broader question: What effect does the method of distribution have on the cost of new equity capital and hence on the minimum rate of return that should be required from investments of these funds?[6]

We can explore the question in terms of the original example we have been using. In that example, the market price per share (M) was $22, the underwriting and flotation costs connected with a direct sale of the new issue was $2 per share, giving the company net proceeds (P) of $20 per share. In this case we argued that the minimum return on investment is appropriately measured by E_A/P or 16.5 percent per annum.

Let us assume that the company decides to sell the shares by issuing rights to stockholders, at the rate of one right to each existing share outstanding, with each right entitling the holder to buy one new share within a stipulated time at a stipulated price below the present market.[7] Let us assume further that this price is $11, that the stipulated period in which the right must be exercised is very short, and that the services of an investment banker are used for the collection and distribution problems involved, for which he is paid at the rate of $1 per share.[8]

What is the cost of capital of new equity funds derived through this particular route? A quick, and wrong, answer would be that the investment should promise at least sufficient returns to maintain earnings per share at the level anticipated without the new investment and the associated financing. This implies a minimum required earning rate of 33 percent[9]—which is twice as high as the 16.5 percent required when capital was derived by direct sale.

The source of trouble in this argument is that it focuses on earnings per share and forgets that in this case earnings per share do not reflect what is happening to the net present worth of owners. The correct approach is to look explicitly at this factor. In order to do this it is useful to distinguish two possible situations. In one, we assume that owners cannot transfer their rights to buy new shares at the privileged price of $11 per share. In the second and the more usual case, we assume that these rights are fully transferable.

Taking the first assumption we have the following situation: Without the investment and the associated financing, the holder of each old share will own $11 in cash plus the present worth of his share in the company which is equal to $22, or a gross total of $33 per shareholding. If the investment is undertaken he has to pay $11 to get an additional share on the privileged basis and after this he owns two shares. If his present worth is not to be impaired by the investment decision these two shares must have a value of at least $33. Since we are still assuming that the earnings added by the proposed investment are of the same quality as earnings already anticipated by the company, it follows that a market value of at least $33 for the two new shares will in turn require earnings of at least $4.95 per two shares.[10] In other words the minimum contribution which the new investment must make in order not to impair owners' present worth is $1.65 per share. Since each new share provides $10 of net investible funds, the minimum required rate is 16.5 percent—the same as when the shares were issued directly. The way the new securities are issued in itself does not affect the cost of equity capital.[11]

We would come to exactly the same conclusion far more simply, by reasoning directly in terms of the net present worth of the company rather than the net present worth of its owners. A proposal will increase the net present worth of a company if its own net present worth is greater than zero, i.e., if its gross present worth exceeds the outlay required. This means it must yield a rate of return greater than the rate at which the market capitalizes earnings of similar quality; i.e., it must yield more than k_e.

What about existing owners who do not have the funds or the inclination to exercise their rights to buy the new shares at $11? If these rights are not transferable they would suffer a loss in wealth, which is offset exactly by a corresponding gain for those shareholders who do exercise their rights. As far as shareholders as a whole are concerned, the appropriate minimum yardstick for screening investment proposals is still 16.5 percent. However, in order to protect the interests of those owners who cannot or may not wish to exercise their rights the sale of these rights is generally permitted. The fact that rights can be sold does not materially affect the required rate of earnings on new investment financed by an equity issue. For those who do exercise their rights to subscribe, the argument is the same as that already outlined: an earning rate on new investment larger than 16.5 percent will increase their present worth above what it otherwise would have been, regardless of where the subscription price is set.

For those stockholders who choose not to exercise their rights but prefer to sell them instead, the argument must be extended to include the value of these rights. Without the proposed investment these shareholders would have owned $22 of value for each original share held. With the proposed investment they will own one original share plus the cash proceeds from the sale of the right. What investment criterion is required to ensure that they too will be better off if the investment is undertaken? To answer this we must first digress to discuss the market value of the right which is sold.

The actual price at which rights will trade obviously depends on numerous factors, such as fluctuations in the market price of the shares, and particular demand and supply conditions for these instruments. But in theory, the value of a right is given by the formula $(M - S)/(N + 1)$ where M is the market value of one old share (with the right attached); S is the subscription price for one new share, and N is the number of rights required to buy each new share. In our example this is $(\$22 - \$11)/2$ or \$5.50. If the company invests its new funds at exactly 16.5 percent, the present worth of shareholders who exercise their rights and buy one new share at \$11 per old share held will be \$33 per shareholding of two new shares. Thus their net present worth is \$22. Shareholders who sell their rights will hold only one new share worth \$16.50, but in addition they will have \$5.50 derived from the sale of each right—or a total net present worth of \$22. For either group net present worth is the same as it would have been without the investment proposal. Hence for either group the appropriate break-even rate on new company investments is 16.5 percent. A lower acceptance rate than this would impair their wealth and a higher acceptance rate would make the company forego an opportunity to increase their wealth. Again, we could have arrived at this conclusion quite simply by measuring in terms of the net present worth of the company, which would lead directly to the answer that k_e is the correct yardstick against which capital-using proposals must be assayed.

NOTES

1. For purposes of this analysis preferred stock is treated as a variant of debt financing.

2. This example is adapted from my earlier paper, "Measuring a Company's Cost of Capital," Journal of Business, XXVIII, 240–52.

3. We have previously defined D, E, and E_A as aggregates, but it is convenient to use the same symbols to express dividends per share and earnings per share.

4. Strictly speaking, the capitalization rate for nongrowth streams is measured by E_A/M where M is the market value per share. The rate E_A/P is slightly higher due to the flotation costs of the new issues.

5. Other factors, independent of the company investment policy, can of course change the capitalization rate. But these factors, such as changes in the level of political, economic, or industrial uncertainty, will bring about a given change in the company's capitalization rate regardless of the particular investment criterion it uses.

6. In general, existing shareholders of common stock have a legal right to subscribe pro rata to any new issue of common stock or other securities which are convertible into common stock. The existence of these preemptive rights is governed by specific provisions in the company's charter or its bylaws or, failing this, by the laws of the state of incorporation and eventually by common law.

Where preemptive rights exist, a shareholder who chooses not to exercise his rights is generally allowed to sell these freely to other parties who want to use them to buy stock at the stated subscription price.

7. More frequently, the conditions of sale require several rights to buy one new share. Our assumption simplifies the arithmetic without affecting the logic of the argument.

8. In practice, the privileged price is rarely set this far below current market price. A discount of 10-15 percent is more common. Also, we have set the fees for collection and distribution underwriting at one-eleventh of the gross price or 10 percent of the net proceeds to the company to keep them identical with the fees assumed in our earlier example. In practice expenses of selling new securities will vary with the mechanics of the sale.

9. There will be twice the number of original shares outstanding. In order to maintain earnings per share, total earnings will have to be at least double the amount expected in the absence of the new investment, i.e., the investment must contribute at least $3,300,000 to future earnings. But the sale of 1,000,000 new shares gives the company net proceeds of only $10 per share or $10,000,000. Hence the minimum rate of earnings required is 33 percent if the rate of earnings per share is not to be impaired.

10. This is based on the capitalization rate of 15 percent, at which the present market ($22) appears to be valuing anticipated earnings ($3.30) of this particular quality.

11. There will be a small, indirect effect if the different routes to new equity issuance have different flotation expenses.

V. THE COST OF RETAINED EARNINGS

Our conclusion, thus far, is that the cost of external equity funds for purposes of capital investment decisions is appropriately measured as $k_e = E_A/P$ where E_A is the flow of net earnings expected without the investment proposal which is being considered, and P is the net market value of existing ownership rights. However, this formulation applies to a highly restricted model in which:

1. Investment proposals within the company are homogeneous with respect to the quality of yield offered.

2. The company is financed entirely by equity funds.

3. True earnings are equal to book earnings, i.e., the amount of depreciation deducted from the cash flow generated by operations is exactly enough to maintain earnings at the anticipated level.

4. This level of earnings contains no upward or downward trend.

In this chapter we retain the first two assumptions but extend the analysis first to the cost of funds derived from retained earnings and later to an examination of situations in which projected earnings contain growth trends of various types.

The Cost of Retained Earnings

Companies derive the bulk of their equity capital from the retention of earnings. Like external equity these funds have no cost in an accounting sense but they do have a cost in that they can be used for purposes other than reinvestment within the company. What is the proper measure for the cost of retained funds and what should be the minimum rate of earnings required on the use of funds from this source?

Introducing retained earnings, and hence the reinvestment of these funds into the analysis opens the door to a discussion of more realistic situations. The same door leads to some of the most difficult problems in financial analysis.

With retention and reinvestment of earnings we can no longer project the stream of earnings at a constant average level. Nor can we measure the capitalization rate k_e as a simple ratio between anticipated earnings and market value. The price-earnings ratio, that favorite tool of practical analysts, is no longer the simple reciprocal of the capitalization rate, and indeed it loses much of its significance. Dividends and earnings have different values and this brings up the question of which of those streams is capitalized in the process of determining market value.

Abstract models are required in order to visualize the various processes, and this involves either the tedious arithmetic of growth and present values or almost equally tedious exercises in algebra, followed by empirical tests of the ideas incorporated in the models. All of this is unavoidable because the subject is complex and difficult. It is necessary because how the cost of capital should be measured and how the minimum rate of required earnings should be set cannot be answered except within a larger framework of valuation and growth.

However, it is helpful to defer the plunge into dynamic situations and to deal first with the cost of retained earnings, in the simplest possible way. We can do this by assuming that the average level of anticipated earnings is constant[1] and considering a decision to use a small part of current earnings for internal investment in assets. We can begin the analysis by ignoring taxes on personal income or capital gains as well as underwriting and brokerage fees. In this simple case, the cost of retained funds is equal to the cost of funds from external equity issues. In the absence of underwriting costs, net proceeds from new equity sales (P) is equal to the market value (M) and the cost of external equity is simply the capitalization rate E_A/M which we will continue to refer to as k_e.

That the cost of retained earnings is also equal to k_e can be argued in either of two ways. Given the simplifying assumptions we have made, both arguments yield identical results, although we will see that there are important differences in underlying logic which emerge when the simplifying assumptions are lifted.

The first, which we can call the personal use criterion, is that the decision to use earnings for additional internal investment rather than for dividend payments should be made only if the internal investment adds more to stockholders' net present worth than they can add themselves.[2] In the absence of personal income taxes, each dollar of dividends received is worth a full dollar to the owners. Therefore each dollar of internal investment within the company is justified only if it adds at least one dollar to the present worth of the shares. Since the quality of additional earnings is the same as the quality of already anticipated earnings, it must follow that the yield on internal investments must be at least $k_e = E_A/M$ if the investment is to add the required dollar of present worth to ownership rights. Another way of saying the same thing is that stockholders are perfectly capable of investing their dividend receipts at a rate equivalent to k_e, either in the same company or elsewhere, and management should deprive them of this opportunity by withholding dividends for internal investment if, and only if, the promised return is at least equal to k_e.

The second approach, which we can call the external yield criterion, is based on another kind of investment alternative open to the company. This is to invest its funds to acquire a majority control in the assets of an operating enterprise, either in the same industry or in a separate industry. In any reasonable market, external investments should be available which offer an earnings yield equal to and having the same degree of certainty or uncertainty as those offered by the company's existing assets. In addition there should be other external investment opportunities, with a different mix of risk and return, which offer an equally attractive package of yield and certainty. The return available on such external investments is appropriately measured by k_e and this represents the minimum rate of earnings required from internal investment or reinvestment proposals.[3]

Thus, if we ignore personal income taxes and brokerage fees, both approaches argue that the minimum standard of performance for the internal investment of retained earnings is given by $k_e = E_A/M$. But one standard is based on what owners themselves can achieve if they receive the funds in the form of added dividends and the other is based on what management can achieve through the external placement of funds.

If we reintroduce personal income taxes the two approaches yield different answers for the minimum rate of return on internal investments. The standard implied by the external yield criterion approach is not affected by the introduction of personal income taxes. The cost of retaining funds for internal investment is the cost of foregoing available external investment opportunities of comparable quality, and this cost can be measured as $k_e = E_A/M$.

However, the standard implied by the personal use approach changes if we take personal income taxes into account. With personal income taxes, each dollar of dividends paid to stockholders is worth something less than one dollar, the shrinkage depending on the marginal tax bracket of each individual owner. Thus each additional dollar of dividend paid adds less than one dollar to the net present worth of owners. For example, if all stockholders were in the 40 percent marginal tax bracket, the present worth of one dollar of earnings paid out is 60 cents. Stockholders can no longer buy a stream of earnings equal to k_e with each dollar they receive. All they can get is a stream equal to $.6k_e$. This line of argument suggests that the net present worth of owners can be increased more if the funds are used for internal investment rather than if they are used for the payment of dividends, even if the yield on internal investments is below $k_e = E_A/M$. For the artifical case of a uniform tax bracket of 40 percent and zero tax rates on capital gains, the use of funds for any internal investment yielding more than $.6k_e$ would be better for owners than the payment of these funds as dividends.

A precise formulation of the cost of retained funds based on the personal use approach presents formidable difficulties if the assumption of uniform tax rates is lifted. When stockholder tax brackets vary from zero to high percentage figures, a precise formulation is impossible. Happily it is unnecessary to pursue these refinements. The proper measure of the opportunity cost of any course of action, in this case the proposed internal investment, is the best alternative opportunity the course of action forces us to forego, and at minimum this is equal to k_e, the yield available on external investment. The exact measure for the next best alternative is not necessary to the analysis. In other words, so long as external opportunities are available, the minimum measure for the cost of internal funds is k_e, regarless of the effect of personal taxes.[4]

It is possible, of course, to envisage situations in which internal investment opportunities and available external opportunities of the kind described fail to exhaust the flow of internally generated funds, i.e., situations in which a company is forced into a decision

between the use of internal funds for investment at some rate
lower than k_e and the use of these funds for dividends payments.
In such rare cases, the personal use criterion may be relevant
as a minimum standard that must be surpassed by any investment,
internal or external, which uses funds that might otherwise be
paid on dividends.[5] Under these unusual circumstances (assuming
that the individual stockholders are in a wide range of personal
income-tax brackets) there may be no determinate solution for
the cost of capital problem.

None of the foregoing analysis is meant to imply that the use
of funds for dividends never represents the most important alternative to internal investment. Nor does it follow that retention
must take place so long as investment opportunities better than
k_e are available. We are here interested only in the investment
decision and in setting a correct standard of performance which
must be exceeded if an internal investment is to be approved.
The way in which the investment, once approved, is financed is a
separate issue. It is quite possible, for example, to envisage a
situation in which an investment passes the screening standard
k_e but will not be financed internally even though these funds are
there, on the grounds that dividends have priority, i.e., that the
cost of using dividends, after some given level of retention, is
somehow too high. The answer in this case is to finance from
external sources. But as far as the investment decision is concerned the appropriate standard is k_e.

Growth Models

We turn now to the problem of measuring the cost of equity
capital, under more dynamic conditions in which the general level
of earnings is expected to rise. Several reasons might lead to
growth in earnings.

1. The simplest reason for anticipating growth is that past or
recent investments are expected to bear fruit and to increase
earnings to a higher level.

A similar situation exists if the reinvestment of funds charged
to depreciation each year is expected to be sufficient not only to
maintain net earnings at current levels but to add to the company's
stock of assets and hence to its earning power.

In both these cases the anticipated growth does not require any
reinvestment of earnings. They can be represented by an expected

net earnings stream which rises for a short period and then levels off again.

2. A second, and very common reason for anticipating growth in earnings is the more or less permanent policy of reinvesting some part of earnings.

It is necessary to distinguish between two separate types of growth financed by reinvestment. One is based on the existence of opportunities to use capital internally at yields that are above normal rates of return. This is a growth situation in the true meaning of the term. It depends on specific but finite opportunities which stem from a company's special and nonreproducible position in technology, manpower, or markets.

A company's opportunity for this kind of growth investment is limited both with respect to the amount of funds that can be invested and the period over which such investments are available. This form of growth cannot be projected indefinitely into the future.

The second and more common situation is properly referred to as expansion rather than growth. Regular reinvestment out of earnings brings about an expansion in assets, earnings, and dividends, but the firm does not foresee specific opportunities to invest funds at higher than normal rates of return.

We will see later that there are good reasons for separating these two forms of expansion, at least for conceptual purposes. We will do so by referring to one situation as true growth and to the second as expansion.

Temporary Growth. What is the basis for measuring the cost of equity capital for a company whose earnings are expected to grow in the future even without any reinvestment of earnings?

The general basis is the same as that used for a company without this form of growth, namely, the capitalization rate k_e implied by the growing stream of anticipated earnings, on the one hand, and the net market value of the stock, on the other. Only the mechanics of measuring this rate are different.

For example, assume a company whose shares are selling at $16 in mid-1960, which anticipates the following stream of net earnings, without the proposed investments under consideration and without any reinvestment of net earnings:

Year	Net Earnings Per Share After Taxes (in dollars)
1961	1.10
1962	1.21
1963	1.33
1964	1.46
1965	1.61
1966 onward	1.77 a year

The capitalization rate k_e can no longer be found by taking the simple ratio of expected net earnings to market value. Instead, the problem of measuring k_e is to find that rate of discount which makes the present value of the anticipated stream of earnings equal to its market value. The solution is a tedious one requiring the use of compound interest tables and a trial-and-error process. Using an annual compounding interval, the answer in the example is that k_e = .10 or 10 percent.[6] The cost of capital for this particular company is also 10 percent because any investment of like quality which offers a higher return will raise the present worth of the company by more than the investment outlay. By the same token, any investment of like quality yielding less than 10 percent will add less to present worth than the capital input it requires, and therefore should not be undertaken.

Long-run Growth. Let us turn to the more complex situations in which the anticipated growth in earnings is accompanied by a reinvestment of part of the earnings stream. We will begin with a brief commentary on the situation we have referred to as expansion rather than true growth, i.e., we will begin with situations in which the firm does not foresee specific opportunities for internal investment that offer anything more than the normal returns associated with general expansion of the economy, product improvements, and cost economies.

While this situation is probably the typical one in the American economy it is peculiarly unsuited for our own task of finding a correct basis for setting a company's cost of capital. The cost of capital question is part of a broader model which assumes a sequence of events that is contradicted by most models of expansion based on earnings retention.

The capital budgeting model envisages a firm which, as of any given date, has some projected level of earnings, some opportunities to invest funds, and a market value, and it focuses on the task of finding that minimum rate of acceptability which will lead the company to optimal investment decisions. These decisions, and associated decisions on how the investment proposals will be financed, determine the level of future earnings, the growth of earnings, and the level of retention out of earnings and of outside financing.

Most expansion models begin with some assumption about dividend policy, and hence about retention and reinvestment rates, and then go on to explore the growth processes which these assumptions generate and the associated relationships between the postulated flow of earnings and dividends, on the one hand, and postulated market value, on the other. It is difficult to ask and answer questions about what a firm should do about accepting vestments and hence about retaining earnings in a context which already includes assumptions about what the firm is doing about these variables.

In spite of these difficulties, the expansion and growth models are a necessary part of the analysis. They represent processes that do go on in the real world and force attention to the underlying problems of the market evaluation of securities. In a very real sense, the problem of market evaluation and the problem of measuring the cost of capital are two facets of the same task.

One of the oldest debates in the area of security evaluation is whether investors capitalize earnings or dividends. Much ink has been spilt on this issue and many regressions have been run. The debate is an empty one. When dividends are equal to earnings no problem exists; when dividends are not equal to earnings, the firm is expanding through the use of retained earnings and in this case neither dividends per se nor earnings per se can provide an adequate basis for measuring the returns which investors capitalize in arriving at a market price.

To take the net earnings stream alone as the basis involves double counting because the assumed growth in net earnings requires the steady reinvestment of part of the net earnings stream. To take dividends alone ignores the gain in capital values which comes from rising dividends, which in turn depends on the flow of net earnings and their reinvestment.[7] A correct model must take into account the anticipated flow of net earnings and the reinvestment of such earnings as is required to achieve the anticipated flow, as well as the benefits from this reinvestment. The nomenclature by which such a model is expressed is secondary. We can refer to it as a dividends and earnings approach or as dividends plus capital gains or as an earnings less reinvestment model. All three amount to exactly the same thing.

A Simple Growth Situation. A useful version of such a model, which requires a minimum of mathematics and is well suited for the task of isolating the appropriate way of measuring the cost of capital, is to postulate the market value V of an all-equity company as the capitalized value V (at the rate k_e) of three component forms of returns.[8] These are:

E = the level of (constant) net earnings expected from existing assets, without further net investments

G = the gross present value of capital gains expected from specific opportunities to invest funds at higher than normal rates of return

R = the reinvestment of net earnings required to achieve G.

As before, we assume a completely debt-free company. Also, we assume that all present and future investments are homogeneous as far as quality of yield is concerned, and that the level of uncertainty they involve is reflected in the capitalization rate k_e.

Let each of the investment opportunities we have postulated provide a rate of return equal to r which is higher than k_e, specifically that $r = mk_e$ where m is larger than unity. Assume that these opportunities allow us to invest R dollars a year at these lucrative rates of return and that $R = bE$ where b is any positive fraction smaller than unity.

The value of G can be computed as follows: The first investment of bE dollars yields a stream of added earnings equal to bEr dollars. The same thing happens each succeeding year. Each of these streams has a present value, as of the year it starts to flow, of bEr/k_e. This is simply the value of the constant perpetual stream discounted at the rate appropriate to its quality. What we have then is a series of investments, each of which has a gross present value equal to bEr/k_e at the time it is made. All of them together have a present value as of today of $(bEr/k_e)/k_e$ or bEr/k_e^2. Thus we have $G = bEr/k_e^2$, or, since we have put $r = mk_e$

$$G = \frac{bEmk_e}{k_e^2} = \frac{bEm}{k_e} \tag{5.1}$$

However, in order to exploit the investment opportunities that add a gross present worth of G to the company, we must invest bE dollars each year. The present worth of these inputs is bE/k_e and so we can say that the net present worth represented by the investment opportunities is:

$$G - \frac{bE}{k_e} \text{ or } \frac{bEm}{k_e} - \frac{bE}{k_e} \qquad (5.2)$$

Having measured the net contribution of the foreseeable investment opportunities we can now measure the total value of the company. This is given by adding the capitalized value of the constant earnings stream expected from existing assets to the capitalized value of the expected investment opportunities. Doing this, we have

$$V = \frac{E}{k_e} + \frac{bEm}{k_e} - \frac{bE}{k_e} \qquad (5.3)$$

Our final equation can be stated in several ways. Combining the first and third elements, we have

$$V = \frac{E(1 - b)}{k_e} + \frac{bEm}{k_e} \qquad (5.4)$$

Since b is equal to the proportion of earnings retained and reinvested, $E(1 - b)$ is equal to the dividend payout from the constant stream, and so we have a dividend and capital gains version of valuation, which can be stated as

$$V = \frac{D}{k_e} + \frac{bEm}{k_e} \qquad (5.5)$$

Alternatively, we can state the model entirely in terms of net earnings data:

$$V = \frac{E}{k_e} + \frac{bE(m - 1)}{k_e} \qquad (5.6)$$

While value can be stated in terms of dividends or in terms of earnings, in the light of (5.5) and (5.6) it is easy to see that neither dividends alone (D) nor earnings alone (E) can provide an adequate valuation formula. The answer to the controversey about whether dividends or earnings determines value is that neither does.[9] When each approach is correctly restated so that it does provide a defensible model, the two models come to exactly the same thing.

This is what we meant when we said that the debate about the dividend theory vs. the earnings theory is an empty one.

It is useful to explore Eqs. (5.5) and (5.6) a little further. If the fraction of earnings retained b is equal to zero, then the second term in each equation disappears, D becomes equal to E, and both equations reduce to a simple version $V = E/k_e$. This is exactly the basis we have been using for our cost of capital measure thus far in the form

$$k_e = \frac{E}{V}. \tag{5.7}[10]$$

The size of the capital gain element in Eqs. (5.5) and (5.6) depends on the amount of capital that can be invested in these lucrative outlets (measured by b), the return on these investments over and above the normal rate k_e (measured by mk_e) and by how long the opportunities are expected to be available (assumed to be perpetual in the example). As m approaches unity, the return on investment $r = k_e m$ approaches k_e. When m is equal to one, $r = k_e$ and Eq. (5.5) becomes:

$$V = \frac{D}{k_e} + \frac{bE}{k_e}$$

$$= \frac{E(1 - b) + bE}{k_e}$$

$$= \frac{E}{k_e}$$

In Eq. (5.6) the second term becomes zero when m = 1 and we also have $V = E/k_e$. In either formulation when $r = k_e$ we are back essentially to the no-growth situation. In other words, true growth, as opposed to mere expansion, is dependent on the existence of opportunities to capture capital gains by investing at higher than normal rates, in this case higher than k_e, thereby creating net present worth over and above the investment outlays required. The virtue of the model we are discussing is that it brings this point out clearly. In fact it ignores what we have called mere expansion, the investment of funds at the normal rate k_e.

There are other purposes for which we might prefer to have a model that traces an expansion process, something the model above does not do. For example, in the last situation discussed, where a company retains and invests a fraction b of each year's

earnings at the normal rate k_e, net earnings and dividends will
expand over time, and it is possible to develop alternative models
for this process. We will consider such a model later. Other similar dynamic models can also be worked out which focus, for example, on investments financed with new equity issues as well as
with retained funds. However, for the present our main interest
in the model presented is to use it as a basis for analyzing the effect of true growth on the capitalization rates and hence on the
cost of capital.

We can do this by restating the equations so that we define the
capitalization rate k_e in terms of the relation between market
values, on the one hand, and earnings and capital gains or dividends and capital gains, on the other. Restating Eqs. (5.5) and
(5.6) we have:

$$k_e = \frac{D}{V} + \frac{bEm}{V} \tag{5.8}$$

$$\text{or} \quad k_e = \frac{E}{V} + \frac{bE(m - 1)}{V} \tag{5.9}$$

The capitalization rate k_e is the overall rate at which the present market value V capitalizes the overall returns promised by
already existing investments and certain specifically envisaged
future investment opportunities that yield more than k_e. It is the
rate of return which stockholders are going to achieve without
any other net investments. From this it follows that any proposed
investment, other than those mentioned above, must offer a yield
at least equal to k_e if it is to benefit present owners, regardless
of whether it is financed externally or internally. In short, the
capitalization rate k_e is the appropriate measure for a company's
cost of equity capital, but it is no longer equal to the simple ratio
between earnings from already installed investments and market
price. It is higher than this rate to the extent that the company
owns or has access to specific investment opportunities which
will create net present worth.

A Dynamic Model: Growth Versus Expansion

We turn now to dynamic models which trace all expansion processes, whether or not they involve true growth as we have defined it. The problem with dynamic processes is that they are
difficult to describe except at considerable length. The outstand-

ing dynamic model presented in recent years, at least in terms of simplicity and clarity, is that by Gordon and Shapiro,[11] and the model we will investigate is based on the approach they use, though not on its detailed content.

Assume a company whose market price is V, which is earning E_o dollars currently and paying D_o dollars in dividends currently. The company proposes to retain a fraction b of its earnings regularly, which it plans to use for internal investments. Assume, for mathematical convenience, that dividends are paid and discounted continuously, and that the discount or capitalization rate is k_e. It can be shown that earnings, dividends, and reinvestment will all grow continuously, at a rate of $g = br$, where r is the rate of return on the reinvestment of earnings. Under these circumstances we have:

$$V = \frac{D_o}{k_e - g} \tag{5.10[12]}$$

The normal procedure in dynamic models is to state the price of a stock as the present value of a growing stream of future dividends with each element in this stream discounted at the rate k_e. This is a long and awkward statement. The formulation given in Eq. (5.10) permits us to reduce this to manageable but mathematically equivalent terms. It states that V, the market value, is equal to the current dividend discounted at a rate $k_e - g$. As in all dividend growth models we must assume that the growth rate g is smaller than the discount rate k_e, or the price of the stock will be infinite.

Solving Eq. (5.10) for k_e we have:

$$k_e = \frac{D_o}{V} + g$$

$$= \frac{D_o}{V} + br \tag{5.11}$$

The capitalization rate k_e is equal to the current dividend yield plus the rate br at which the dividend stream is expected to grow. The growth rate itself depends on the proportion of net earnings devoted to reinvestment and the rate achieved on these reinvestments. It is useful, as before, to distinguish between growth situations in which r is greater than k_e and expansion situations in which this differential does not exist.

In the equilibrium case, where $r = k_e$, we have an expansion situation and the capitalization formula in the dynamic model gives exactly the same results as the simple earnings model or the simple growth model we discussed earlier in which $k_e = E_o/V$. The proof of this is as follows:

$$V = \frac{D_o}{k_e - g} \qquad\qquad \text{[from Eq. (5.10)]}$$

but $D_o = E_o(1 - b)$, and $g = br = bk_e$ when $r = k_e$. Substituting these values of D_o and g in Eq. (5.10) we have:

$$V = \frac{[E_o(1 - b)]}{[k_e(1 - b)]}$$

$$= \frac{E_o}{k_e}$$

or $\qquad k_e = \dfrac{E_o}{V}$

In other words, if special growth opportunities are not foreseen, the cost of capital suggested by this formulation amounts to the same basic measure $k_e = E/V$ we have been using in static situations. Expansion as such does not affect our basis for setting the minimum rate of return required.

How about the case where r is smaller than k_e? The case is a contradiction: if the company cannot invest funds internally at k_e or better it should not be investing these funds. There is no point in asking what the proper minimum investment standard is for situations which assume that the company firmly intends to follow an investment policy which breaches this standard.

When we turn to the true growth situation, in which the investment rate r is higher than k_e, we meet the fact that the simple growth model presented earlier and the dynamic model being discussed cannot be compared because of basic differences in the amount of growth they assume. The growth model assumes that the firm is able to invest a constant dollar amount each year (equal to a fraction b of this year's net earnings) in special high-yielding projects. The second, or dynamic model, as we have called it, assumes that such investment takes place at an expanding rate (equal to a fraction b of the expanding stream of earnings). Even if a common rate of return on these investments is assumed, the amount of net capital gains available will be greater under the second assumption. The bigger the values assumed for b and r, the greater the difference between the two models.

For example, let us assume that $E_o = 10$, $D_o = 6$, $b = .4$, $k_e = .10$, and $r = .20$. The last assumption implies that the special investment opportunities offer a rate of return twice as high as that regarded as normal for earnings of this quality, i.e., $m = 2$. In this case the valuation formula used by the dynamic model $V - D_o/(k_e - g)$ gives us $V = 6/(.10 - .08) = 300$.

The different assumption made by the earlier simple growth model yields a much smaller answer for V_o, as it should do. This is:

$$V_o = \frac{D}{k_e} + \frac{Ebm}{k_e} = 60 + 80 = 140.$$

It would be convenient to remove the differences in underlying assumptions which lead to these different results. This can be done, but the simplicity of one or the other models will be destroyed in the process of making these assumptions conform to one another.[13] As they stand, each serves a different purpose well.

The numerical differences caused by the assumed differences should not hide the essential conceptual similarities between these two ways of looking at a growth situation.

As far as valuation is concerned, we can see these similarities better if we state the valuation formula in the dynamic model as:

$$V = \frac{D}{k_e} + Vbm \qquad\qquad (5.12)[14]$$

This compares directly with the simple growth formula,

$$V = \frac{D}{k_e} + \frac{Ebm}{k_e} \qquad\qquad [\text{from Eq. (5.5)}]$$

Both formulations divide the total value V into two parts. One part is the capitalized value of dividends, equal in both formulations to 60 if we assume the numerical values given in our last example.

The second part is the net present worth of capital gains expected from growth investments. This is much larger in the dynamic formulation, because it assumes much larger opportunities.

Most important of all, there is no third segment of value in either formulation which ascribes any value to mere expansion of

earnings, i.e., any rise in future earnings due to a simple reinvestment at normal rates of return k_e.[15]

The similarities between the two formulations can also be seen
from the cost-of-capital point of view. In the dynamic case we
have:

$$k_e = \frac{D}{V} + g$$

$$= \frac{D}{V} + bmk_e.$$

In the simple growth model we had:

$$k_e = \frac{D}{V} + \frac{bmE}{V}.$$

Both capitalization rates contain a basic component equal to
the current dividend yield and both add a second or growth component, which contains similar but not identical variables. Since
the numerical differences due to the alternative assumptions made
are reflected in the different values of V assumed, there will be
no numerical differences in k_e if the appropriate value of V is used
in each case.

In the real world all we have is one market value. Which formulation should we use in measuring the capitalization rate as a
guide to the company's cost of equity capital? Neither formulation is universally applicable.

The simple growth model begins with specific anticipations
about future earnings, without expansion, from existing assets
(an estimate required by any cost-of-capital model). It postulates
and measures limited foreseeable opportunities for the company
to invest funds at above normal rates, the amount of such investment, and the probable rate of return. These two pieces of information, in conjunction with the market value of shares, provide
the basis for setting the cost-of-capital for all other proposed investments. In brief, the formulation comes close to being a rational capital-budgeting model: invest only if this investment will
increase net present worth over what it is otherwise anticipated
to be.

The dynamic model begins with current earnings and dividends
and projects a rate of growth for these variables, assuming a rate
of dividend payout and assuming a rate of return on the amount of
annual reinvestment implied by this predetermined payout ratio.

This procedure may well be closer to corporate practices. It may also provide a useful basis for estimating some other company's cost of capital. But it does not tie in as well with the capital allocation principle which visualizes reinvestment as a result of profitability, rather than the other way around.

NOTES

1. In this context the word "constant" refers only to the long-run level of the earnings stream and does not imply the absence of short-run movements around this level.

2. Management does not always have a free choice in dividing earnings between dividend payments and internal investment. Some portion of earnings may be due to inventory profits from price rises and hence are automatically tied up within the source from which they are derived. Likewise there may be other preexisting restraints on the availability of cash for dividend payments. Our discussion concerns only that segment of earnings about which management does have a choice.

3. Strictly speaking, this applies only to external assets in which the company can acquire a sufficient ownership interest to permit a consolidated return for purposes of corporate income taxation. A minority interest in external assets will offer the company a net after-tax yield which is lower than k_e.

4. This analysis contradicts the position I took in an earlier paper, "Measuring a Company's Cost of Capital," Journal of Business, XXVIII, 240-52, in which I argued personal taxes did affect the cost of retained funds in principle but that the diversity of shareholder tax brackets precluded the use of any measure except k_e.

5. Since external portfolio investment opportunities (i.e., opportunities to acquire a minority interest in the common stock of other companies) which offer a gross yield equivalent to k_e are available in amounts far in excess of the residual internal funds of any one company, the minimum external yield available is at least as high as $.48k_e$ (assuming a 52 percent corporate tax). Thus the personal use criterion becomes operative as a standard only if the marginal tax bracket of the average or typical stockholder is assumed to be below 52 percent.

6. The mechanics of the solution are discussed in a later chapter. In the example given, the expected stream of growing earnings has a present value of $16 only if it is discounted at a rate of 10 percent.

7. Needless to say, those who use valuation formula based solely on current earnings or solely on current dividends are doubly wrong.

8. It is more convenient sometimes to deal in company aggregates than on a per share basis.

9. Except of course when dividends are equal to earnings, in which case either is correct and the argument vanishes.

10. Except that E and V refer to company aggregates rather than to amounts per share.

11. Gordon and Shapiro, "Capital Equipment Analysis: The Required Rate of Profit," Management Science, III, 102-10. The classical treatment of the subject of growth models is Williams, The Theory of Investment Value.

12. In the discrete case, k_e is the value which satisfies

$$V = \sum_{t=1}^{\infty} \frac{D_t}{(1 + k)^t}$$

In the continuous case we have:

$$V = \int_0^{\infty} D_t\, e^{-kt}\, dt$$

But $D_t = D_o e^{gt}$ (i.e., the dividend grows at the continuous rate g). Substituting this in the equation above, we have:

$$V = \int_0^{\infty} D_o e^{gt}\, e^{-kt}\, dt$$

$$= D_o \int_0^{\infty} e^{-t\,(k-g)}\, dt$$

$$= \frac{D_o}{k-g}$$

13. We could make the expansion model conform to the growth model by assuming that only \$4 a year are invested at the 20 percent rate and that the rest of retained earnings are invested at k_e or 10 percent. Alternatively, we could assume a growing volume of reinvestment in the growth model. Such models would have to be more complex than the ones we have used.

14. Since $V = D/(k_e-g)$, from eq. (5.10) and $g = br = bmk_e$, we have $D = V(k_e - bmk_e)$, or $V(1-bm) = D/k_e$, or $V = D/k_e + Vbm$.

15. There is an especially important lesson in this for people who use price/earnings ratio and who might fail to distinguish between true growth and mere expansion of earnings (which adds nothing to stockholders' wealth that it does not take away through retention).

VI. THE COMBINED COST OF DEBT AND EQUITY

Thus far we have analyzed the cost of capital under the assumed condition that the firm is financed entirely by equity. We must now lift this assumption and introduce the use of other forms of capital.

Our first problem is that nonequity funds can be derived in many ways. These range from pure debt to forms of preferred stock which come close to resembling equity itself. Between these extremes there is a spectrum of hybrid financing arrangements which incorporate different mixtures of priority, flexibility, fixity, maturity, and yield. Relative to pure equity, all of these sources of capital have a prior but more limited claim to income (and generally to assets in the event of insolvency).

The introduction of many kinds of capital means that there are several central questions to be faced rather than just one. It is helpful to break the over-all problem into four component facets.

1. Given conditions in the capital markets, and given an existing mixture of financing, how should we measure a company's cost of capital for purposes of investment decisions? We will refer to this as the cost of capital problem.

2. Given the general structure of rates in the capital markets, how does the mixture of funds with which a company is financed affect the level of a company's cost of capital? We will refer to this as the leverage problem.

3. Is there some optimum structure of capitalization at which the cost of capital is minimized? This is the problem of optimal capital structure.

4. Finally, given a company's cost of capital and a set of investment decisions based on this cost, how should the company finance the investment it decides to undertake? This is the problem of financing policy.

The first facet, the cost of capital problem, is concerned with how investment proposals should be assayed, i.e., with setting a company's minimum required rate of return so that the right set of investment decisions will be made. For the simplest situation, in which the company maintains a given capital structure, the answer to the cost of capital question does not depend on our answer to the second question. But if a company is in the process of changing its capital structure by increasing or decreasing the proportion of debt used, we cannot arrive at a theoretically correct solution to the cost of capital problem without first solving the second question.

The second question, the leverage problem, is explicitly concerned with how the company's cost of capital is altered when its capital structure is changed. The answer to this question is still the subject of considerable controversy. Because the general solution to the cost of capital problem itself depends on the answer we give to the leverage problem, the measurement of the cost of capital is also at least partially unsettled. So, too, is the problem of capital structure.

The answer to the fourth problem depends in part on the way in which the first three problems are answered and on the investment decisions to which they lead. But policy with respect to year-to-year financing has other determinants as well. We will therefore defer our discussion of financing strategy to the final chapter of this book.

Business Uncertainty and Financial Uncertainty

With the introduction of debt to the analysis we must distinguish between net operating earnings, or the return on total capital employed, and net earnings, the amount available to owners after interest charges on borrowed funds have been paid. As before, we will define net operating earnings as total "cash" earnings less whatever capital-consumption allowances are required to maintain the flow of cash earnings at the projected level.

In the all-equity case net operating earnings and net earnings are equal and we have used the symbol E for both. We must now differentiate between the two; we will refer to anticipated net operating earnings as O and retain the use of E for expected net earnings. The fact that interest payments on borrowed funds are tax-deductible expenses introduces a minor complication, which we will avoid for the time being by assuming that corporate income taxes do not exist.

The quality of the expected stream of net operating earnings O depends on a complex of factors which we can refer to as business uncertainty. These factors include general expectations with re-spect to over-all economic and political trends, specific expecta-tions about the particular regions and markets within which the company acquires resources and sells its products, and the speed and flexibility with which the company can lower its total operating costs when total revenues decline. All three factors interact, and their combined effect determines the level of uncertainty or quality which is attached to anticipations about the future flow of net op-erating earnings. In the case of an all-equity company, net earn-ings E have the same quality as net operating earnings O.

The use of debt interposes a fixed charge between an uncertain stream O and the stream of residual earnings E. This reduces the certainty or increases the degree of uncertainty of the flow E rel-ative to that of the flow O. In addition, the use of debt exposes equity holders to a potential loss of their total equity in the com-pany's assets in the event that O is not sufficient to cover the fixed charges to creditors. Thus, when debt is used there are two rea-sons for postulating some decline in the quality of the residual flow of net earnings E relative to the quality of the flow O. The quality of O depends only on the level of business uncertainty in-volved. The additional uncertainty is caused by the financing pol-icy used and we will refer to it as financial uncertainty.[1]

The use of borrowed funds affects both the quantity and quality of anticipated net earnings, generally in opposite ways. One effect of investing borrowed funds, also referred to as trading on the eq-uity or leverage, is that owners get to keep all investment returns in excess of the fixed contractual rate at which funds are borrowed. If the rate of return on total investment is higher than the rate of interest, the rate of return on the equity component of investment will be higher than the rate of return on total investment. But this increase in the quantity of net earnings per dollar of owner-funds is achieved only at some sacrifice in the quality of these returns. In an uncertain world, the presence of a prior fixed charge re-duces the certainty of residual net earnings below the certainty of operating earnings.

It is helpful to look at the problem of quality in terms of the specific market capitalization rates through which the quality or uncertainty of different kinds of income streams are reflected. In order to simplify the analysis we will assume that this struc- ture consists of only two kinds of capital—pure equity and pure debt. We will also assume that expected earnings flows do not contain any growth trends and that all existing and proposed in- vestments are homogeneous with respect to quality of yield. Fi- nally, we will ignore the effect of corporate income taxes during many phases of the analysis.

Let us assume that Company X has the following characteris- tics:

Market values

B = the market value of bonds outstanding	$ 5,000
S = the market values of stock outstanding	$ 5,000
V = the total market value of the firm	$10,000

Earnings flows

O = annual net operating earnings expected	$ 1,000
F = annual interest charges on debt[2]	$ 200
E = annual net earnings on equity	$ 800

For this company we must have the following relationships: $V = B + S$, i.e., the total market value of the company is equal to the total market value of bonds plus the total market value of stock. Also, ignoring the effect of capital income taxes for the time being, we have: $O = E + F$, i.e., total anticipated net operating earnings will be divided between bondholders and stockholders, with a fixed amount F going to the creditors and the residual amount E going to owners.

We can therefore think of three streams of income and three capitalization rates at which these are valued. Assuming that streams E and O contain no growth element, we have:

$$B = \frac{F}{k_i} \text{ or } k_i = \frac{F}{B} \qquad (6.1)$$

$$S = \frac{E}{k_e} \text{ or } k_e = \frac{E}{S} \qquad (6.2)$$

$$V = \frac{O}{k_o} \text{ or } k_o = \frac{O}{V} \qquad (6.3)$$

The first rate, k_i, is simply the effective yield on the company's bonds. It is the rate at which the market capitalizes the most definite form of return that the company offers.

The third rate, k_o, reflects the basic business uncertainty of the company, i.e., it reflects the quality of the stream of operating earnings O. The rate k_o will be higher than k_i because the chances that the company will actually earn the anticipated amounts are lower than the chance that it will earn at least some fraction of this amount—namely, the fraction required for service charges on the debt.

Finally, the rate k_e is the rate at which the anticipated residual flow to owners is assayed. In an all-equity situation k_e will be equal to k_o. With some debt in the financing structure, the residual flow is subject not only to business uncertainty but to the additional financial uncertainty caused by borrowing.

For any company, with any capital structure, we have $k_e > k_o > k_i$. In terms of our numerical example we have: $k_i = .04$ or 4 percent; $k_o = .10$ or 10 percent; $k_e = .16$ or 16 percent. For any capital structure the relationship among the three rates at any point of time is given by:

$$k_o = \frac{k_e S + k_i B}{B + S} \tag{6.4}$$

This relationship follows from the basic relationships given in Eqs. (6.1), (6.2), and (6.3) and is independent of whichever of the various alternative approaches to valuation we choose.[3] The rate k_o can also be stated as a weighted average of k_e and k_i. Let $w_1 = S/(S + B)$ be the equity proportion of total market value and $w_2 = B/(S + B)$ the debt proportion. Since $w_1 + w_2 = 1$, Eq. (6.4) can be written:

$$k_o = k_e w_1 + k_i w_2 \tag{6.5}$$

This states that the overall or combined capitalization rate k_o is the weighted average of the cost of equity capital k_e and the cost of debt funds k_i with the stock and bond components of total market value used as weights.

In terms of our numerical example we have: $k_o = (.16)(.5) + (.04)(.5) = .10$. It is also possible to express the equity capitalization rate k_e in terms of the overall capitalization rate k_o plus an adjustment for financial uncertainty:

$$k_e = k_o + (k_o - k_i) \frac{B}{S} \tag{6.6}$$

In this formulation the adjustment for financial uncertainty is equal to the debt-equity ratio times the spread between k_o and k_i.

Equation (6.6) is also a direct extension of the basic relationships of Eqs. (6.1), (6.2), and (6.3) and the relationship it states is independent of any valuation approach we choose.

In terms of our numerical example we have: $k_e = .10 + (.10 - .04) \cdot 1 = .16$.

Measuring the Cost of Debt and Equity

We can turn now to the problem of measuring the cost of a mixture of debt and equity funds. Let us begin with the simplest possible case in which a company has a given capitalization structure which it intends to maintain, i.e., it finances new investments with capital derived in the same proportion as that already existing. We will assume, as before, that the benefits promised by new investments are of the same quality as those expected from existing assets.

Our task is simply to find the "cost" of a joint package of funds which combines debt and equity in given proportions. In our example this proportion is 50 percent debt and 50 percent equity.

The intuitive answer to this problem, and this is also the correct answer, is that the cost of capital k can be measured directly by measuring k_o or less directly by taking the combined weighted cost of debt and equity $k_e w_1 + k_i w_2$. Since $k_o = k_e w_1 + k_i w_w$, both measures yield identical results.

We can test this answer in terms of a specific investment proposal. Assume that a proposal under consideration offers to yield net benefits equal to ΔO per annum on a total investment of C dollars or a rate of return equal to $\Delta O/C$ per annum. We are assuming that these benefits have the same quality as the yields expected on existing assets. Hence the gross present worth of the proposal is given by $V = \Delta O/k_o$. In order for a proposal to be acceptable V must be larger than C. But V will be larger than C only if $\Delta O/C$ is larger than k_o. Hence k_o is the appropriate measure for the minimum rate of return that should be required on new investment proposals which offer returns of the same quality as those promised by existing assets. Thus, the condition for acceptance of new investment can be stated:

$$\frac{\Delta O}{C} > k_o \qquad\qquad (6.7)$$

An alternative and more familiar way of measuring k, the minimum required rate of return, is in terms of $k_e w_1 + k_i w_2$. Using this formulation we have as our condition for acceptance:

$$\frac{\Delta O}{C} > k_e w_1 + k_i w_2 \tag{6.8}$$

A third formulation reasons in terms of the net earnings promised by a proposal relative to the net amount of equity investment required. This approach would reason as follows:

Capital investment required	C
Amount to be financed by debt	$C \cdot w_2$
Amount to be financed by equity	$C \cdot w_1$
Net operating earnings promised	ΔO
Interest charges on debt used	$C \cdot w_2 k_i$
Net earnings promised	$\Delta O - Cw_2 k_i$
Rate of net earnings on equity investment	$\dfrac{\Delta O - Cw_2 k_i}{Cw_1}$

The minimum acceptance level is given by the condition:

$$\frac{\Delta O - Cw_2 k_i}{Cw_1} > k_e \tag{6.9}$$

This condition gives exactly the same results as those given by the first two formulations. This is so because the net return on equity investment will exceed k_e if and only if $\Delta O / C > k_o$. This can be shown as follows: If

$$\frac{\Delta O - Cw_2 k_i}{Cw_1} > k_e$$

then

$$\Delta O - Cw_2 k_i > Cw_1 k_e$$

and

$$\Delta O > Cw_1 k_e + Cw_2 k_i$$

and

$$\frac{\Delta O}{C} > k_e w_1 + k_i w_2$$

The symbolic expression for the last formulation is awkward but it presents no corresponding difficulties when actual numerical estimates are involved.

Problems of Measurement and Application

Each of the three formulations of the minimum acceptance standard has its own peculiar virtues. The first formulation, in which the cost of capital is defined directly in terms of k_o, has the advantage of simplicity. It has the additional advantage that it directly relates the minimum required rate of return to the level of business uncertainty involved in the investment. So long as we are dealing with simple situations in which we ignore some of the complexities of the real world it provides the most convenient basis for measuring the investment criterion.

However it is difficult to extend this formulation to situations in which the simplifying assumptions are removed. The formulation itself loses much of its simplicity in the process and what is more important it cannot handle many of the variations found in the real world.

Once we get away from the restrictive assumptions we have been using, there are at least three factors which must be included in the analysis. These are:

1. Corporation income taxes and the deductibility of interest and lease payments in computing tax liabilities.[5]

2. The fact that individual investment proposals will offer returns which differ in quality from those offered by existing assets or those offered by other new proposals.

3. The fact that individual investment proposals permit different access to debt financing and permit it at different rates.

Under these more realistic conditions it would be wrong to apply a single over-all rate k_o as the standard against which all proposals are assayed. We need to adjust for differences in uncertainty between the returns offered by the individual investment proposals and the average uncertainty reflected in k_o. This means we cannot use the same k_o as the standard for all proposals. One way of getting around this difficult problem is to use a single acceptance rate k_o but to "handicap" the benefits offered by each individual proposal in some fashion to eliminate the difference in quality between it and the aggregate earnings expected on all assets now held. Unfortunately, we know little about how to apply these adjustments or about how k_o itself varies with uncertainty. Nor are we likely to find out much more.[6]

Our third formulation of the cost of capital, which uses k_e as the standard against which to judge the rate of net returns to

equity expected from investment proposals, offers a more prom-
ising vehicle for handling the complex situations we are now discussing. The tax factor can be taken into account quite directly by
computing both the expected returns to equity and k_e itself on an
after-tax basis. It can also handle the fact that different proposals
should be charged different rates of interest, depending on the actual rates at which borrowed funds are available. The evidence
suggests that these variations are not insignificant.[7]

In addition, the k_e formulation provides a basis for judgment
when we encounter the task of adjusting for the different degrees
of uncertainty inherent in the different uses of funds being considered.

The rate k_e reflects the combined effect of business uncertainty
and financial uncertainty contained in the expected equity yield on
existing assets. Each new asset under consideration offers operating earnings whose quality may differ from that reflected in k_o.
By "allowing" each new proposal a different proportion of debt
financing varying from zero to high proportions of debt, it is possible to adjust the overall level of business plus financial uncertainty contained in any given proposal so that the net yield it offers
can be compared directly against the overall uncertainty reflected
in k_e.

Taking the tax effect into account, the basis for acceptance is
provided by an adaptation of the third formulation given in Eq. (6.9).

$$\frac{(1 - t)(\Delta O - Cw_2 k_i)}{Cw_1} > k_e (1 - t) \tag{6.10}$$

In Eq. (6.10), t is the rate of corporate income tax, w_2 is the debt
ratio which equates the overall uncertainty (business plus financial) of the net earnings promised by the proposal to the overall
uncertainty of expected net earnings on existing assets, and k_i is
the actual rate of interest payable on funds borrowed for the proposal. A specific rate may or may not exist. If it does, it should
be used. If it does not, the appropriate measure for k_i is the average rate of interest payable on all existing debt.

This solution is neither objective nor perfect. Indeed it relies
heavily on judgment. But it does provide a useful conceptual
framework within which judgment can be exercised. At worst it
gives us an acceptance standard which is identical to that given by
the k_o formulation. But in general it is likely to provide a more

accurate basis for screening the many different kinds of uses to which company funds may be put.

NOTES

1. Frequently referred to as leverage, financial risk, or internal risk. See Mayer, "Analysis of Internal Risk in the Individual Firm," The Analysts Journal, XV, 91-95.

2. We are ignoring the effect of corporate income taxes.

3. Equation (6.4) is derived as follows:

$$k_o = \frac{O}{V} = \frac{E + F}{B + S}$$

But $E = k_e S$ [eq. (6.2)], and $F = k_i B$ [eq. (6.1)]. Hence

$$k_o = \frac{k_e S + k_i B}{B + S}$$

4. From eqs. (6.1) and (6.2) we have

$$k_e = \frac{E}{S} = \frac{(O - F)}{S}$$

But $O = k_o V = k_o(B + S)$ and $F = k_i B$. Hence

$$k_e = k_o \frac{(B + S) - k_i B}{S}$$

$$= k_o S + \frac{(k_o - k_i)B}{S}$$

$$= k_o + (k_o - k_i)\frac{B}{S}$$

5. For an extension of the k_o formulation which takes the effect of corporate income taxes into account, see Modigliani and Miller, "The Cost of Capital, Corporation Finance, and the Theory of Investment," American Economic Review, XLVIII, 261-97.

6. Ibid., p. 267.

7. At any point of time, rates charged may vary by type of asset (loan rates, mortgage rates, equipment rates, rates implied by lease agreement, equipment, trust rates, and the like) as well as by location and duration of the asset.

VII. THE COST OF NEW BORROWING

In the last chapter we discussed the problem of measuring the cost of capital under the condition that the firm maintains a given capital structure. We must now turn to the more difficult problem of how to measure the cost of capital when the increment of financing used consists of new borrowing alone or contains a different mixture of debt and equity than that contained in existing capitalization. In other words, how does our measure of the company's cost of capital change with changes in the degree of leverage employed?

We can bring this problem into focus by assuming that a company which has given degree of leverage in its existing capital structure decides to finance this year's capital budget entirely with debt funds. What minimum rate of return should it require on the investments proposed within the budget? To simplify the issue, we will restore the assumption that all investment proposals offer returns of like quality and equal in quality to those offered by existing assets. Also, we will ignore the effect of corporate income taxes and the fact that interest payments are deductible in computing taxable income.

One possible answer to the cost of capital question is that the cutoff rate which should be used is simply equal to the nominal cost of borrowed funds, i.e., the specific charges payable for the use of debt, or k_i, in the terminology we have been using.

Computing this cost is an uncomplicated matter. The borrowing contract generally stipulates a precise timetable for the repayment of principal and interest. The net proceeds of the loan or bond flotation are also known. The effective rate k_i is that rate which equates the required payments to the net proceeds. The only other adjustment required arises from the tax deductibility of interest charges, which we are abstracting from for the present.

The trouble with this approach is that it ignores a second form of "cost" associated with increasing the ratio of debt to equity. This is the deterioration which increased borrowing brings about in the quality of residual net earnings, i.e., the increase in financial uncertainty. This cost is much harder to compute, but it cannot be ignored.[1]

Nobody, to my knowledge, has explicitly advocated the use of the interest rate as the minimum financial standard against which the uncertain returns promised by new investment proposals should be screened.[2] The use of the interest rate as a cutoff point for internal investments in economic theory is a different matter and assumes that the return on investment is measured in terms of its certainty-equivalent.

All the solutions put forward in an uncertainty context suggest that some allowance should be made for the effect of increased leverage on the quality of net earnings. The difficult question, which has not been fully answered, is: How much allowance should be made? Regardless of how our measure for the cost of capital is formulated, a complete answer to the measurement question depends upon a defensible answer to another question, namely: How does a change in leverage change the set of capitalization rates at which the market values the various income streams generated by a company?

The three formulations outlined in the preceding chapter still hold, but the values to be assigned to the capitalization rates will depend upon what effect changing leverage is assumed to have on these rates. In other words, the formulations themselves are completely independent of the valuation approach used. The minimum acceptance standard for new investments which we plan to finance entirely with debt is still given by any one of the following formulations: the rate of net operating earnings contributed by the investment must exceed k_o; the rate of net operating earnings contributed must exceed $(k_e w_1 + k_i w_2)$; or the rate of net earnings contributed by the equity investment required $(\Delta O - Cw_2 k_i)/Cw_1$ must exceed k_e. But the proposed change in leverage will change w_1 and w_2 and may change k_o, k_e, and k_i, and it is the new values of these variables that are relevant in measuring the cost of capital. These in turn depend upon which theory of valuation we hold.

Leverage and Capitalization Rates

Leverage (L) can be defined in many different ways. Staying with the simplifying assumption that the firm uses only two kinds of capital, pure debt and pure equity, we can measure leverage as:

$$L = \frac{B}{S}$$
the ratio of debt to stock, at market prices[3]

$$L = \frac{B}{(B + S)}$$
the ratio of debt to total capital, at market prices[3]

$$L = \frac{F}{O}$$
the ratio of debt charges to net operating income.

Some measures are more convenient for certain purposes and some, for others. For the present we will use the first of these alternatives and measure L as the ratio of bonds to stocks, with both values computed at market prices.

The heart of the valuation question is what happens to k_e, k_o, and k_i as the degree of leverage is changed. To get at this we need to compare the level of k_e, k_o, and k_i at one capitalization structure with their level at some different structure, with all other factors constant. Since the principal controversy concerns the change in k_e and k_o, we will assume, to begin with, that k_i remains constant, i.e., the rate of interest paid by the company on borrowed funds does not change with changes in leverage. We will also assume that the general structure of rates in the capital market remains constant.

We can isolate the effect of leverage on k_e and k_o in either of two ways. One way is to compare k_e and k_o for two otherwise identical companies which have different capital structures. Alternatively we can take a single company and ask what happens to k_e and k_o when leverage alone is changed. Both devices are useful, but it is easier to begin with the first.

Let X and X* be two companies with identical assets, each of which is expected to generate net operating earnings O and O* of identical size and quality. For numerical purposes let us assume that O = O* = \$1,000 per annum. Let X be an all-equity company. Hence expected net earnings E is equal to net operating earnings O. Assume that the market capitalizes these earnings at the rate k_e equal to .10 or 10 percent. Thus the total market value of Company X is O/.10 or \$10,000. Since X has no debt outstanding, the total market value of its stock is also \$10,000.

The second company, X*, is financed with debt as well as equity. Specifically, it has \$3,000 or 4 percent bonds outstanding on which it pays interest at \$120 per annum. Assume that the present effective yield k_i on bonds of this quality is also 4 percent. Thus B*, the market value of the bonds, is \$3,000. To simplify the issue we assume that corporate income taxes do not exist.

We can now get to the question at issue. What is the value of S*, the stock of Company X*, and what rates of capitalization k_e* and k_o* are implied by our answer to this question? There is as yet no settled solution.

One school of thought analyzes the value of X* as follows:

Net operating earnings O*	\$ 1,000
Interest on debt F*	\$ 120
Net earnings expected on equity E*	\$ 880
Assumed equity capitalization rate k_e*	.10 or 10 percent
Market value of stock S*	\$ 8,800
Market value of bonds B*	\$ 3,000
Total value V*	\$11,800
Implied over-all capitalization rate k_o* .08475 or $8\frac{1}{2}$ percent[4]	

This is frequently referred to as the net income approach to security evaluation.[5] The name is descriptive, but it is also deceptive. The core of the approach is not that it gets at value by capitalizing net earnings (or net income), but that it capitalizes net earnings at a constant given rate (in this case, 10 percent) regardless of the degree of leverage used, at least up to some leverage level regarded as moderate or acceptable.[6]

At the other extreme we have the net operating income approach to valuation. This analyzes the value of Company X* differently.

Net operating earnings O*	\$ 1,000
Assumed capitalization rate k_o*	.10 or 10 percent
Market value of company V*	\$10,000
Market value of debt B*	\$ 3,000
Market value of stock S*	\$ 7,000
Implied equity capitalization rate k_e* .1257 or $12\frac{1}{2}$ percent[7]	

The two approaches give very different results and hence lead to different answers to the cost of capital question and to the "correct" acceptance standard for new investments.

The net income approach assumes that increased leverage brings about no deterioration in the quality of net earnings and no

increase in the rate at which these net earnings will be capitalized
by the market, at least so long as borrowing is confined to amounts
below some acceptable limit. This implies that the market value
of a company (bonds and stocks) increases with leverage at least
up to some acceptable limit of leverage beyond which the equity
capitalization rate rises rapidly with subsequent increases in the
degree of financial uncertainty imposed by further increases in
leverage. For example, assume that X* had used $5,000 in bonds
instead of just $3,000 and that this amount of borrowing is within
acceptable limits, then according to the net income approach its
value would have been $13,000 instead of $11,800.[8] At this level
the implied value of k_o^* would be .769.

The assumption that k_e remains constant over the relevant
range of leverage must imply that k_o falls as leverage is increased.
The rate at which k_o falls is given by the basic relationship $k_o =$
$k_e w_1 + k_i w_2$. This relationship holds for all levels of leverage or
for all approaches to valuation.

The general effect of leverage on capitalization rates, according
to the net income approach to valuation is shown in Figure 1 below. The data in the diagram assumes that the acceptable limit of
leverage, measured as the ratio of B to S, is .625.[9] Beyond this
level of leverage, k_e and k_i rise rapidly. Below it, k_e and k_i are
both invariant with respect to changes in leverage.

The net income approach is rarely put forward in the unquali-
fied form shown in Figure 1. This extreme version, in which k_e
is strictly constant over some acceptable range of leverage, is
simply one limiting version of the various approaches to valuation.

The opposite limit is given by the net operating income approach, shown in Figure 2. This approach assumes that k_o is a
constant. Since the relationship $k_e = k_o + (k_o - k_i)B/S$ must hold,
assuming k_o is constant means that k_e must rise as leverage rises.
This implication is that any increase in the ratio of net earnings
on equity brought about by the use of "low-cost" debt is exactly
offset by the deterioration in the quality of these net earnings
such that the total market value of the company is constant for
all capitalization structures.

Between these two extreme versions we have a gradation of approaches which suggests that a judicious use of leverage has only
a moderate effect on k_e. The implication of this is that so long as
the use of leverage is confined to limits acceptable by the capital
markets, the rise in k_e is not sufficient to offset the increase in

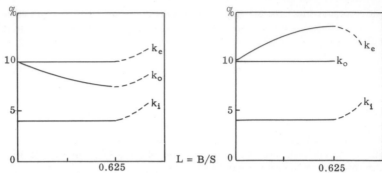

Fig. 1: Leverage and Capital-
          ization: the Net Income
          Approach

Fig. 2: Leverage and Capital-
          ization: the Net Operating
          Income Approach

the rate of net earnings on equity achieved by the increased use
of low-cost debt. By and large, this is the traditional view.[10] Its
implications are shown in Figure 3.

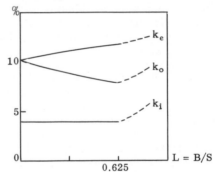

Fig. 3. Leverage and Capitalization:
          the Intermediate Approach

Implications for Cost of Capital. The effect of leverage on capitalization rates and values is of central importance for the question of selecting an optimal capital structure. But it also has implications for measuring the cost of capital for a company which
plans to derive and increment of financing entirely from debt
sources, i.e., for a company which is planning to change its capital structure. We can examine these implications in terms of a
specific example.

For purposes of numerical illustration let us take the company whose characteristics were outlined in the preceding chapter. For this company we had:

$$k_i = \frac{F}{B} = \frac{2,000}{5,000} = .04$$

$$k_o = \frac{O}{V} = \frac{1,000}{10,000} = .10$$

$$k_e = \frac{E}{S} = \frac{800}{5,000} = .16$$

and

$$L - \frac{B}{S} - \frac{5,000}{5,000} - 1.00$$

So long as the company maintains its present capital structure, the appropriate measure for its cost of capital k is given by k_o or by $k_e w_1 + k_i w_2$. Both measures are identical and set the minimum required return on new investment (of identical quality) at 10 percent.

Alternatively, we can use the third formulation in which the basis for acceptance of an investment proposal is the condition that the net earnings promised by the proposal on the net equity investment it requires must exceed k_e.

Let us assume that the company has an investment proposal which offers a yield of ΔO on an outlay of $1,000 which it proposes to finance entirely by borrowed funds. What is the correct measure for the minimum required return? We will assume that the quality of net operating earnings promised by the proposal is the same as that expected from existing assets.

The theoretical answer is that the appropriate basis for decision is given by any one of the three formulations examined earlier:

1. The rate of net operating earnings offered by the proposal, in this case, $\Delta O/1,000$, must exceed k_o^*.
2. This rate must exceed $k_e^* w_1^* + k_i^* w_2^*$.
3. The rate of net earnings offered by the proposal on the net equity investment required, in this case, $\Delta O - 1,000 \cdot w_2^* \cdot k_2^* / 1,000 \cdot w_1^*$ must exceed k_e^*.

Although the formulations for the cost of capital are exactly the same as those used earlier, the appropriate values for k_e, k_o, k_i, w_1, and w_2 (denoted above by asterisks) are those which will prevail under the revised capitalization structure. It is against these new values that the proposed investments must be assayed. In other words, the correct sequence of analysis is first to estimate what values k_e, k_o, and so on will have after the proposed change in capitalization, but without the new investment, and then to examine the merits of the proposed investment against these new values of k_e and k_o.

In practice, the proceeds of the new borrowing will be used for financing the new investment, or else the borrowing itself will not be undertaken. But, for analytical purposes, we need to deal separately with the two operations involved: (a) the change in leverage and (b) the investment decision. In order to achieve this analytical separation we can assume that the funds derived by borrowing $1,000 are used to buy $1,000 worth of outstanding common stock. This will change the degree of leverage and this in turn will affect the values of k_e, k_o, and the like. For convenience we will continue to assume that k_i is constant. The net operating income approach would analyze the effect of leverage as follows: k_o remains the same, i.e., the new $k_o^* = .10$; L, the degree of leverage, will rise from $B/S = 5,000/5,000 = 1.0$ to $(B + 1,000)/(S - 1,000) = 6,000/4,000 = 1.5$; k_e will rise with the increase in leverage. The rate of rise is given by the basic relationship $k_e = k_o + (k_o - k_i)B/S$, from which we get $k_e = .10 + (.06)(1.5) = .19$. Also, w_1, the equity proportion, will fall from .5 to .4; w_2, the debt proportion, will rise from .4 to .5. The combined cost of capital will be $k_e^* w_1^* + k_i^* w_2^* = (.19)(.4) + (.04)(.6) = .10$, which is the same as it was before the change in leverage.

On the basis of this reasoning, the three formulations for the investment criterion would be:

1. $\Delta O/1,000$ must exceed k_o or 10 percent,
2. $\Delta O/1,000$ must exceed $k_e^* w_1^* + k_i^* w_2^*$ or 10 percent,
3. $\Delta O - w_2 \cdot k_i \cdot 1,000/1,000 \cdot w_1$ must exceed k_e^* or 19 percent

Under any of the formulations the new proposal must promise to increase net operating earnings by at least $100 in order to justify the required investment of $1,000.

The rationale for the conclusion that this is the correct minimum is as follows. The quality of the operating earnings offered by the new investment is the same as that of existing assets. Hence the increment in net operating earnings will be capitalized by the market at the same rate. Since the approach assumes that this rate k_o is unaffected by the change in leverage, it uses a rate of .10 for capitalizing the promised increment in net operating

earnings. At this 10 percent rate a proposal requiring an outlay
of $1,000 will add to the net present worth of the company only
if the increment in operating earnings it offers exceed $100.

A different approach to valuation will yield a different criterion
for the new investment decision because it makes a different assumption about what happens to k_e, k_o, and so on, when leverage
is increased.

For example, a proponent of the extreme version of the net
income approach to valuation would argue that the increase in
leverage would have the following effect:

B rises from $5,000 to $6,000.
Interest payments rise from $200 to $240.
Net earnings decline from $800 to $760.
But k_e remains the same (assuming of course that the
increase in leverage is within acceptable limits),
i.e., $k_e^* = .16$.

The value of stock left outstanding is given by 760/.16 or $4,750.[11]

The total value of the company rises to $10,750.
w_1, the equity proportion falls from .5 to .44186.[12]
w_2, the debt proportion rises from .5 to .55814.
L, the degree of leverage rises from 1.0 to 1.2632.
k_o falls with the increase in leverage such that
$k_o^* = k_e^* w_1^* + k_i w_2^* = (.16)(.44186) + (.04)(.55814) = $
.0930.

The combined cost of capital also falls to .0930 or 9.3 percent.

On the basis of the net income approach to valuation the minimum required rate of return on new investment financed entirely
by borrowing is 9.3 percent. Alternatively, the rate of net earnings promised by new investment on the equity capital required
(assuming a debt ratio of .558) must exceed 16 percent, the equity
capitalization rate k_e which is assumed to be unchanged.

Intermediate approaches to the valuation question will give a
minimum investment criterion somewhere between the 9.3 percent rate implied by the net income approach and the 10 percent
rate of the net operating income approach.

Which is correct? This depends, of course, on which valuation
approach is correct and unfortunately there is no clear-cut answer
to this issue. There is, in fact, no convincing way in which this
question can be answered. The answer itself has important impli-

cations for general decisions on capital structure and also for the
purpose of utility rate-making decisions in which the question of
a fair rate hinges in part on the assumed relationship between
leverage and capitalization rates.

However our immediate problem is to find an appropriate way
of measuring the cost of capital for investment decisions. As far
as this issue is concerned, the debate about which valuation approach is correct is not of great practical significance. It would
be preferable to have a clear-cut solution to the valuation question—but an acceptable working basis for measuring the cost of
capital is available even in the absence of such a solution. This
answer is to compute the cost of capital on the basis of the existing capital structure and the values of k_e, k_o, and others associated
with this structure regardless of how the increment of funds is financed.

The suggested answer sidesteps the unsettled valuation debate.
But it is not as brash as it might appear to the purist. Leverage
is not ignored. Any effect which leverage has on capitalization
rates is automatically incorporated into the suggested measure of
capital cost, if, as, and when this effect occurs. The only thing
which the measure ignores is the anticipated effect of small future
changes in leverage attributable to each intended increment of financing. This effect is small if not trivial. It must be remembered
that the computation of a company's cost of capital and its use as a
screening standard rest heavily on estimates—of future earnings
on existing assets, of anticipated growth, of expected earnings
from specific proposals, and of the levels of uncertainty associated
with each expectation. In this context, any sacrifice in accuracy
caused by ignoring the anticipated effect of each small increment
of financing on over-all leverage and hence on capitalization rates
is negligible.

NOTES

1. It is possible to envisage a third category of cost attaching to the
use of borrowed funds. These are restraints on managerial freedom
imposed by the lenders as a condition of the loan. For analytical purposes it is convenient to lump these in with the increase in financial
uncertainty.

2. An exception is the hypothetical treasurer in the famous Liquigas Case. See Pearson Hunt and Charles M. Williams, Case Problems in Finance, revised edition (Homewood, Ill., Richard D. Irwin, 1955).

3. Alternatively we could use book values in these measures.

4. From $k_o^* = \dfrac{O^*}{V^*}$.

5. See Durand, "The Cost of Debt and Equity Funds for Business: Trends, Problems of Measurement," in Conference on Research in Business Finance.

6. Our example assumes that the amount of leverage used by Company X* is well within this "acceptable" range.

7. From $k_e^* = \dfrac{E^*}{S^*} = \dfrac{880}{7,000} = .1257$.

8. We obtain $13,000 as follows:

Net operating earnings	$ 1,000
Debt	$ 5,000
Interest on debt	$ 200
Net earnings	$ 800
Assumed capitalization rate	.10
Value of stock	$ 8,000
Total value of stocks and bonds	$13,000

9. If leverage is measured as to ratio of B to total capitalization B + S, the acceptable limit would be .385. One of the dangers of graphic or visual analysis of these relationships is that different definitions of leverage on the horizontal axis result in different shapes for the k_e and k_o curves. For example, in Figure 1, k_o is a falling curve which flattens as we move from left to right. If leverage were measured differently, k_o would follow a different path. Thus, if leverage were defined as the ratio of B to total capitalization, k_o would be a straight downward-sloping line.

10. See, for example, Benjamin Graham and David L. Dodd, Security Analysis, 2nd edition (New York, McGraw-Hill, 1940), chs. 39-40, especially p. 542. Also, Harry G. Guthmann and Herbert E. Dougall, Corporate Financial Policy, 3rd edition (Englewood Cliffs, New Jersey, Prentice-Hall, 1955), p. 245, in which the authors write: "The use of low-yielding prior securities has made it possible to offer a higher return on the common stockholders' investment and so increase its attraction. Theoretically, it might be argued that the increased hazard from using bonds and preferred stocks would counterbalance this additional income and so prevent the common stock from being more attractive than when it had a lower return but fewer prior obligations. In practice, the extra earnings from trading on equity are often regarded by investors as more than sufficient to serve as a 'premium

for risk' when the proportions of the several securities are judiciously
mixed.''

11. Since we are assuming that the $1,000 derived by new borrowing
is used to redeem $1,000 of stock previously outstanding, the value of
$4,750 implies that the increase in leverage increases the market value
of shares still outstanding.

12. The new values of w_1, w_2, and L differ from those given in the
net operating income example because the two approaches make different assumptions about the way stock prices change, and this affects
the value of w_1, w_2, and L. The numerical estimates shown in each illustration are derived by carrying out the valuation argument of each
approach.

VIII. LEVERAGE AND THE COST OF CAPITAL

Anticipating the effect of a change in leverage on capitalization rates is not of great consequence as far as the pragmatic task of measuring a company's cost of capital is concerned. But it is an issue of central importance for the problem of determining a firm's capital structure, i.e., the composition of the credit side of its balance sheet.

There are two ways in which the problem of determining financial structure can be approached. One viewpoint is essentially dynamic. Each year, or each period, the firm faces a financing problem which it presumably solves by selecting some optimal combination of the various sources from which funds are available. The choice it makes will depend on its own policies with respect to dividends and retention; on current capital market conditions; on expectations with respect to the cost and availability of funds in future periods; and on expectations regarding the volume and quality of earnings from existing assets and planned additions to assets. Taking this view the over-all financial structure at any point of time is simply the result of sequential decisions made in the past. In other words, the concern of this approach is optimal financing decisions; financial structure as such is largely a by-product of the continuous and continuing process of matching sources to uses in the light of emerging developments in business and capital market conditions.

The alternative approach to the problem of financial structure is essentially static. Given prevailing conditions in the capital markets, and given some existing structure of assets and the quantity and quality of earnings these are expected to yield, is there some optimal financial structure which the firm should adopt which is somehow superior to alternative financial structures available?

Both ways of looking at the problem of financial structure are

important, and in practice financing decisions and decisions about
financial structure are made jointly. But for purposes of analysis
it is useful to separate the two, and in doing so, it is convenient to
deal first with the static problem of locating the optimal financial
structure for a given set of conditions.

Financial structure itself has many dimensions. One of these
is financial leverage, the mix of debt and equity employed. This
chapter and the next are concerned with the effect of leverage on
the cost of capital. The following chapter will deal with the other
characteristics of a firm's financial structure.

Optimal leverage can be defined as that mix of debt and equity
which will maximize the market value of a company, i.e., the aggregate value of the claims and ownership interests represented
on the credit side of its balance sheet. Thus the problem of leverage is part of the broader problem of achieving the optimal usage
of economic resources, namely that of finding the best combination of inputs for any given structure of output, in the light of prevailing market conditions and prices.

The advantage of having an optimal financial structure, if such
an optimum does exist, is two-fold: it maximizes the value of the
company and hence the wealth of its owners; it minimizes the company's cost of capital, which in turn increases its ability to find
new wealth-creating investment opportunities. We can also look
at these same advantages from the social point of view. An optimal financial structure makes better use of society's fund of capital resources, and thus it increases the total wealth of society.
Also, by increasing the firm's opportunity to engage in future
wealth-creating investment it increases the economy's rate of investment and growth.

What is optimal financial structure? How can it be defined in
terms of leverage? This question leads us directly back to the
valuation problem we left unresolved in the last chapter.

Leverage and Market Values—The Traditional View

The heart of the leverage question is given by the following
question: Given that a firm has a certain structure of assets,
which offers net operating earnings of given size and quality, and
given a certain structure of rates in the capital markets, is there
some specific degree of financial leverage at which the market
value of the firm's securities will be higher than at other degrees
of leverage?

The traditional answer to the question is that there is such an optimum point or range. But like all "traditional" answers, this one is not easy to define. Discussions of the leverage effect are generally mixed in with a discussion of other elements in the financial structure, with observations of the kinds of financial structure used by various industries, and with a discussion of the determinants of the financing question (age of company, managerial reputation and conditions in the capital markets, the need for flexibility, and the like). Even when a question of the optimal use of leverage, as such, is discussed in normative terms, the prescriptions given are relatively vague and unsupported by analysis or evidence.

But implicitly, or more rarely, explicitly, traditional doctrine assumes that there does exist an optimal point of leverage for any given firm. The objective may be stated as "a balanced capital structure (which) observes the proper relationship between debt and equity," [1] or as one adapted to the level of business uncertainty involved: "It is clearly logical that the greater the inherent business risk, the less should be the financial risk, the thicker should be the equity, and the less the leverage." [2] Among the more specific statements on the subject of optimal leverage are those by Graham and Dodd, and Guthmann and Dougall, referred to in the preceding chapter.[3] In addition, the traditional view is reflected in numerous pronouncements by utility commissions on the subject of optimal or desirable levels of leverage. [4]

Translated into the terminology we have been using the traditional position is that other things being equal, the market value of a company's securities will rise as the amount of leverage L in its financial structure is increased from zero to some point determined by the capital market's evaluation of the level of business uncertainty involved. Beyond this point and up to a second point, changes in leverage have very little effect, i.e., within this range of leverage, the total market value of the company is unchanged as leverage changes. Beyond this range of "acceptable" leverage the total market value of securities will decline with further increases in L.

Even if we take just two types of capital, debt and equity, the posited relation between market value and leverage is the joint result of many factors. To keep the analysis straightforward we will deliberately ignore the effect of corporate taxes. It is convenient to state the general interactions envisaged by the traditional viewpoint in terms of the notation developed earlier. In this nota-

tion S is the total market value of a company's stock, E is expected
net earnings, and k_e is the rate at which the market capitalizes
these net earnings; B is the total market value of bonds, F is equal
to interest charges on debt, and k_i is the effective yield on the company's debt; O is net operating earnings and k_o is the overall capitalization rate which equates O to the company's total market value
$V = S + B$; $w_1 = S/V$ and $w_2 = B/V$.

The traditional view of the hypothetical reaction of a firm's
total market value as leverage is increased from zero is that there
are three discernible phases involved.

1. During the first phase, increasing leverage increases market value. In this phase, k_e, the rate at which the market capitalizes net earnings, rises with increasing leverage but does not rise
fast enough to offset the increase in the net earnings rate achieved
through the increased use of lower cost debt capital. For most of
this range the cost of borrowing k_i is either constant or rises only
negilgibly because actual and potential creditors regard the debt
proportions involved as being within sound limits. The combined
effect of increasing leverage on F, E, k_i, k_e, w_1, and w_2 is such
that total market value $V = (E/k_e) + (F/k_i)$ rises. A corollary of
of this is that the combined cost of capital $k_e w_1 + k_i w_2$ falls with
increases in leverage. Since $k_o = k_e w_1 + k_i w_2$ the overall capitalization rate k_o also falls as leverage rises.

2. After a certain degree of leverage is reached, further moderate increases in leverage have little or no effect on total market value. During this middle range the changes brought about on
F, E, k_e, and k_i offset one another so that total market value $V =$
$(E/k_e) + (F/k_i)$ remains virtually constant as leverage is increased. Likewise, the combined cost of capital $k_e w_1 + k_i w_2$ and
the overall capitalization rate k_o are also virtually constant.

3. Beyond a certain critical point, still further increases in
leverage are unwise. The reaction of the capital market will be
such that k_e and k_i rise rapidly. And this results in a fall in V and
a rise in $k_o = k_e w_1 + k_i$.

A numerical illustration of the kinds of relationships envisaged
by the traditional point of view is shown in Table 1 and the accompanying Figure 4. These data are for a company at a given point
of time with assets, earnings expectations, and capital market
conditions taken as given. They present hypothetical changes similar to those posited by the traditional view on the effect of leverage on the individual variables.

Table 1. Leverage, Market Values, and Yields

B	k_i	O	F	E	k_e	S	V	k_o	L_1	L_2
0	4	100	0	100	10	1,000	1,000	10.0	0	0
100	4	100	4.0	96	10	960	1,060	9.4	.10	.09
200	4	100	8.0	92	10.3	893	1,093	9.1	.22	.18
300	4.2	100	12.6	87.4	10.8	810	1,111	9.0	.37	.27
400	4.5	100	18.0	82.0	11.5	711	1,111	9.0	.56	.36
500	5.0	100	25.0	75.0	12.3	611	1,111	9.0	.82	.45
600	5.5	100	33.0	67.0	13.1	512	1,111	9.0	1.17	.54
700	7.0	100	49.0	51.0	14.0	364	1,064	9.4	1.92	.65
800	8.5	100	68.0	32.0	15.0	213	1,013	9.9	3.76	.79
900	?	100	?	?	?	?	?	?	?	?
1,000	?	100	?	0	-	0	B	?	∞	1.00

B = amount of debt (market value)
k_i = effective interest rate paid (percent)
O = annual net operating earnings expected
F = annual interest charge
E = annual net earnings expected
k_e = equity capitalization rate (percent)

S = market value of stock
V = total market value (S + B)
k_o = over-all capitalization rate (percent)
L_1 = leverage defined on B/S
L_2 = alternative definition of leverage B/(B + S)

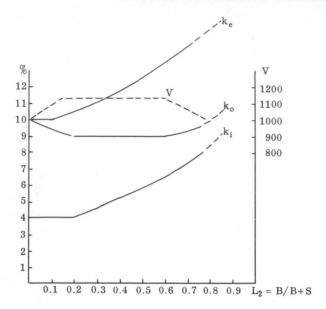

Fig. 4. Leverage, Market Values, and Yields

The diagram measures leverage in terms of L_2, the ratio of bonds to total capital (at market value). Between $L_2 = 0$ and $L_2 = .27$, market value rises and k_o falls with increases in L_2. Between $L_2 = .27$ and $L_2 = .54$, the market value and k_o curves are horizontal, as the various effects of increasing leverage offset each other. Between $L_2 = .54$ and $L_2 = .80$, increases in leverage lower market value and raise the cost of capital k_o. The fourth phase covering values of L_2 above .80 has been left blank, because what happens at these extreme ranges is rarely discussed in this particular context.[5]

The traditional position on leverage is frequently referred to as a U-shaped cost of capital curve. The k_o curve developed in the illustration is a fairly shallow saucer with a horizontal section over the middle ranges of leverage. We have drawn it this way because the basic relationships are such that it is extremely difficult to envisage a k_o curve that does not have these characteristics.

Where the cost of capital function does have a horizontal phase, this represents the range of optimal leverage. Where the cost of capital function is actually U-shaped, the precise location of the optimal degree of leverage is the precise point where the rising marginal cost of borrowing is equal to the average overall cost of capital. For this purpose the marginal cost of a unit of debt capital must be measured as the sum of two things: (a) the increase in total interest payable on debt capital when debt is increased from B to B'; (b) the amount of extra net earnings required to restore the value of the equity component to what it would have been under the pre-existing capitalization rate k_e which prevailed before debt is increased from B to B'. Thus in the example the marginal cost of borrowing the seventh $100 unit of funds is given by $49 − $33 = $16 (the increment of total interest involved) plus $3 (the amount of extra net earnings which would make up for the loss in stockholder net wealth caused by a rise in k_e from 13.1 to 14 percent). If $19 is the total cost of borrowing $100, then the marginal cost, expressed as a rate, is 19 percent. The average cost of capital at this point is only 9 percent. Hence the use of more debt, at this leverage level, increases the average cost of capital. In short, the marginal cost of capital and the U-shaped average costs are related in the same general way that all marginal and U-shaped average curves are related. The marginal curve is below the average curve when the average is falling; it is above the average when the average curve is rising, and it is equal to the average when the average is at its lowest point. This point corresponds to optimal leverage and this optimum can be located through an examination of the relation between the marginal cost of debt at various levels of leverage and the average cost of capital at these levels.[6]

The actual location of the optimum leverage point or range for any given firm will vary with the amount of business uncertainty involved in its operations and with the attitude of the capital markets toward this uncertainty. This in turn is made up of the composite of expectations with regard to a company's product markets and prices, the fixity of its costs, the liquidity and marketability of its assets, and the opinion of the market with respect to the firm's management. As far as those elements of instability and uncertainty are concerned, a firm is likely to resemble other firms in the same industry. But interindustry differences are likely to be significant. Because of this, each industry group can be expected to have a different optimum range as far as leverage is concerned.

This optimal range occurs at a higher level of leverage for stable industries than for unstable industries.

One kind of evidence in favor of the traditional position is that companies in the various industry groups appear to use leverage as if there is some optimum range appropriate to each group. While significant intercompany differences in debt ratios exist within each industry the average usage of leverage by broad industry groups tends to follow a consistent pattern over time. However this kind of observation in itself is not proof that an optimum leverage structure actually exists. Convincing proof that a company is actually better off, in the sense that it has a higher market value or a lower overall cost of capital, at one level of leverage rather than another is hard to find. Those who make sport with regressions have yet to show that the traditional position on leverage as it has been outlined above is either proven or contradicted by the empirical evidence available.

Several writers have expressed doubts about the logic of the traditional view and the associated thesis that a change in leverage, in itself, can increase a firm's total market value or reduce its overall cost of capital. In one of the earlier papers on the subject of cost capital Durand argued against this thesis because it implies that the totality of risk or uncertainty incurred by all security holders of a given company can be altered by changing the way in which this totality is distributed among the various classes of securities.[7] According to Durand's position and the net operating income approach to valuation which he advocates, a change in leverage can only change the way in which operating earnings and the attendant uncertainty of these earnings is distributed between bondholders and owners: it cannot change the total amount of earnings or the total amount of uncertainty. And since the market value of a company depends on these totals, leverage in itself cannot change total market value.

However, Durand also argues that an optimal point of leverage does exist because the tax treatment of debt and imperfections in the capital market can result in a higher market value for the same totality of risk (and hence a lower cost of capital) when the company uses a judicious mixture of debt and equity.

A more vigorous denial of the traditional position on leverage is that contained in an important and controversial paper by Modigliani and Miller, published in 1958.[8] Their conclusion is that, apart from tax considerations, financial structure, as such, has no influence whatever on a company's cost of capital.

The Modigliani-Miller Thesis

The basic proposition on which the Modigliani-Miller argument rests is that, in a world of perfect markets and rational investors, two identical companies, i.e., two sets of assets offering net operating earnings of the same size and quality, must have the same total market value, regardless of differences in leverage. Given this proposition, the market value of a company and hence its cost of capital are both independent of its financial structure.

Since a perfect market is defined as one in which two identical commodities cannot sell at two different prices, the proposition itself can hardly be untrue. But Modigliani and Miller have a stronger string to their bow. They also show that the capital markets are sufficiently perfect to ensure this proposition. Hence, except for the imperfection caused by the deductibility of interest payments in computing corporate income taxes, the mixture of debt and equity used has no effect on the overall cost of capital.

Specifically, they demonstrate that the ability of investors to engage in personal or "homemade" leverage is enough to ensure that corporate leverage in itself cannot alter total market value, except for the tax-effect factor. Assuming that taxes can be ignored, and assuming further that the yield curve[9] is the same for all borrowers, whether persons or companies, they show that any discrepancy between the market value of two identical assets will be erased by a process akin to arbitrage. From this they infer that leverage can have no effect whatever on market values.

The "proof" is best stated in terms of a simple numerical example. For purposes of this example we will assume that the rate of interest is equal for all borrowers. To begin, we will also assume that it does not vary with the degree of leverage used.

Take two companies, X and X*, identical in all respects except their use of leverage. X is an unlevered company financed entirely by equity. It offers net operating earnings of $1,000 per annum which the market capitalizes at a rate $k_o = .10$. The value of the company is therefore $10,000 and since there is no debt outstanding the value of its stock is also $10,000.

The second company, X*, has $3,000 or 4 percent bonds in its financial structure. We will assume the effective market rate of interest k_i is .04 so that the bonds have a market value of $3,000. The Modigliani-Miller proposition, or the net operating income approach, as we have called it, would argue that the value of Company X* must be the same as the value of Company X, that is, $V* = V = 10,000$.

The traditional approach would set V* at something other than $10,000. If the leverage used by Company X is within the "acceptable" range the traditional theory would place V* > $10,000. For illustrative purposes let us assume a value of $11,000. Since the value of bonds B* is $3,000, the value of stock S* according to traditional theory would be $8,000.

Modigliani and Miller show that this assumed discrepancy between V and V* cannot exist. If it did, it would be erased by what they call arbitrage.[10] The owner of the "over-valued" stock, in this case, X*, the levered stock, could sell his holdings, borrow on his own, buy stock X, and end up with a net gain. In numerical terms the process would go as follows.

Assume that we hold one-tenth of Company X* stock. This holding yields net operating earnings of $100 and on this the company pays interest pro rata amounting to $12. This leaves net earnings of $88.

If the value of S* is $8,000, as suggested by the traditional hypothesis, we can sell our shares in X* for $800. We can then borrow $200 from a broker at 4 percent and use the $1,000 we now have to buy one-tenth of the outstanding stock of unlevered Company X. This new holding would give us net operating earnings of $100 of the same quality we had on our original holding. We pay the broker $8 in interest and end up with net earnings of $92. This is higher than the $88 we would have expected from our previous holding in X*. Furthermore, since the two streams of net operating earnings are of like quality, the fact that the new holding is subject to smaller prior charges makes it better in quality as well as quantity.

The argument is that investors will sell X* and buy X on margin and that this process of arbitrage or switching will continue until the opportunities for further gain are erased. And this will happen only when V* = V.

A similar line of reasoning can be used to show that the total market value of a highly levered company cannot be lower than that of a less levered company.

To illustrate, let us assume that Company X, the unlevered company, is selling at a premium relative to Company X*, the levered or, in this case, the supposedly overlevered company. Specifically, let us assume that the total market value of X* is $9,000 or 10 percent below the total market value of Company X. Since X* has bonds outstanding with a market value of $3,000, S* will be $6,000.

In this situation X is the "over-valued" company. An owner of
one-tenth of X, who expects to get net operating earnings of $100
(and since there are no debt charges, net earnings are also $100),
can sell his holdings and use the $1,000 he gets to buy a mixture
of the bonds and stocks of Company X*, dividing his $1,000 between
debt and equity. To keep the arithmetic simple, assume he buys
$600 worth of stock and $400 worth of bonds of Company X*. The
stock would give him a one-tenth share in the net operating earnings of Company X*, or $100. The company would have to pay $12
of interest on the debt it owes, leaving him with $88 of net earnings.
But his $400 worth of bonds would bring him $16 in interest, so
that the switch on the whole gains him $4 on balance plus some
improvement in quality. The gain available by switching from Company X stock to a mixture of Company X* securities will induce
investors to do so. And this will alter their relative market values,
till once again equilibrium is restored. This will happen only when
$V = V*$.

From this line of reasoning, Modigliani and Miller conclude that
$V = V*$ and $k_o = k_o*$, and hence that for any given company both its
total market value V and the over-all capitalization rate k_o at which
its earnings are valued by the market will be constant over all possible ranges of leverage. This means that the cost of capital function with respect to leverage is horizontal and not saucer-shaped
or U-shaped as previsen by traditional theory. An optimal degree
of leverage does not exist, i.e., there is no such thing as a judicious
mix of debt and equity which minimizes a company's cost of capital
or maximizes its total value. In other words, A.T. & T. would be
just as well off with DuPont's financial structure and vice versa.
It is difficult to assess the significance of the Modigliani-Miller
propositions because more than one issue is involved.

As a model which describes the admittedly artificial world of
perfect markets, their conclusion that leverage cannot change total
market value (and hence the over-all cost of capital) is indisput-
ably true. But since a perfect market is defined as one in which
this conclusion must hold, the model does not tell us very much.
What it says in effect is that in a perfect market the market value
of assets is determined either by earning power or liquidation
value, that the market value of total claims against assets cannot
be different than the market value of the assets themselves, and
that the mere restructuring of claims against the assets cannot
alter market value. This is identical to the basic postulate of the
net operating earnings approach to valuation although Modigliani

and Miller have restated the model more explicitly than anyone else had done before. However the conclusion follows so closely from the definition of a perfect market that nobody familiar with economic reasoning is likely to disagree with it.

When we move from the perfect market model to one a little closer to reality, their finding that the conclusion of the perfect market model holds is no longer either obvious or indisputable. Much of the controversy ushered in by their paper concerns the realism or lack of realism of the intermediate model within which their analysis is set, in which they show that arbitrage is sufficient to ensure the proposition that market value is independent of financial structure.

In particular, three aspects of the simple arbitrage model have been questioned.

1. It ignores the tax-deductibility of interest payments. Modigliani and Miller are perfectly aware of this institutional complication. Indeed they show explicitly that because of it, k_0 is not constant with respect to financial structure but declines steadily as leverage is increased.[11]

2. It ignores the difference between corporate debt and personal debt, i.e., it assumes that personal and corporate leverage can be regarded as equivalent. The criticism is that this is not true for several reasons. For one, companies have limited liability whereas individuals do not: hence the risk associated with owing a given sum of money because of share ownership in a levered company is not the same thing as the risk involved in owing the same amount personally. For another, margin regulations limit personal borrowing power, and many of the major institutional investors (such as pension funds, trust accounts, mutual funds, university endowment accounts, and similar funds) are simply not permitted to engage in "homemade" leverage. A further complication is that the rate charged on personal borrowing does not vary with the overall amount of leverage involved, i.e., a person can borrow at a given rate regardless of whether he buys a highly levered stock or an unlevered one.

Again Modigliani and Miller are aware of these institutional complications, but they do not agree that it affects their argument in any significant way. They point out that by and large, the rate charged on brokers' loans has been approximately the same as the rates charged on corporate borrowing. They also point out that the arbitrage argument requires only that some investors en-

gage in these equilibrating transactions. Finally they point out
that margin borrowing is not the only way in which an individual
investor can alter his aggregate leverage or risk position:

"Under normal conditions, moreover, a substantial part of the
arbitrage process could be expected to take the form, not of having the arbitrage operators go into debt on personal account to
put the required leverage into their portfolios, but simply of having them reduce the amount of corporate bonds they already hold
when they acquire underpriced unlevered stock. Margin requirements are also somewhat less of an obstacle to maintaining any
desired degree of leverage in a portfolio than might be thought at
first glance. Leverage could be largely restored in the face of
higher margin requirements by switching to stocks having more
leverage at the corporate level." [12]

It has also been argued that the arbitrage argument ignores the
fact that an investor holding a levered issue can increase his net
yield just as fast by borrowing as an investor holding an unlevered
issue, and therefore that price differences between two similar issues with different levels of corporate leverage will not be erased
by arbitrage based on adding leverage. This argument misses the
main point of the Modigliani-Miller argument because it ignores
the fact that increased homemade leverage on an already levered
corporate stock injects more uncertainty into the holding. What
the arbitrage argument tries to do, and quite rightly, is to compare
two situations in which uncertainty is "equalized" by allowing each
holding a given total amount of corporate and personal leverage.

In spite of the institutional complications the weak point of the
Modigliani-Miller argument is not its postulate that increasing
leverage cannot increase market value. It is true that corporate
interest is tax-deductible and that companies may be able to borrow at net rates and conditions which are less onerous than those
available to indivduals. But even if these complications are taken
into account their proposition would still produce results that are
considerably different from those envisaged by the traditional hypothesis of a shallow U-shaped curve. Indeed, instead of a constant k_o curve, and the associated finding that financial structure
does not matter at all, the Modigliani-Miller proposition amended
to take the the tax-deductibility of interest into account would
postulate that k_o declines continuously as leverage is increased,
and the recipe for optimal leverage associated with this is that
companies ought to be financed 99.9 percent with pure debt!

This brings us to the second facet of the Modigliani-Miller proposition:

3. Financial structure, no matter how extraordinary, cannot decrease market value. This argument ignores the attitudes of lenders and its effect on lending rates. In a perfect market, lenders presumably behave as rationally as investors, i.e., a truly perfect market requires a variety of hidden assumptions, not only about the relation of k_e to k_o but also about the relation of k_i to k_o and k_e. In fact there is considerable evidence that even if the equity market and the debt market are each perfect or nearly perfect within themselves, the securities market as a whole is highly imperfect, i.e., that cross trading between the two markets is seriously hindered by institutional attitudes and legal restraints. There is nothing in the arbitrage argument which will ensure that levels of k_i and k_e will be "equilibrated" in any sense. If it is a fact that k_i at various levels of leverage for any particular company is independent of k_o and k_e, it is entirely possible for a company to reduce its market value through behavior which the debt market regards as unacceptable. We will see later why this is true and therefore why the amount of debt used is not a matter of indifference. Meanwhile it is necessary to turn first to a brief discussion of the empirical tests which have been used for the purpose of isolating the apparent shape of the k_o curve under different leverage conditions.

NOTES

1. See W. Bayard Taylor, Financial Policies of Business Enterprise, 2nd edition (New York, Appleton Century Crofts, Inc., 1956), p. 233.

2. See Waterman, "Financial Leverage," in Essays in Business Finance, p. 105. See also Burtchett, Corporation Finance (New York, Harper and Brothers, 1934), p. 355 for specific numerical prescriptions of how leverage should be tailored to business risks.

3. Chapter VII, note 10. Other explicit statements that judicious leverage can increase the total market value of a firm's securities are contained in Eiteman, "Promotion," in Essays on Business Finance, pp. 11-12; and S. M. Robbins, Managing Securities (Boston, Houghton Mifflin, 1954).

4. See, for example, United States Federal Communications Commission, The Problem of the "Rate of Return" in Public Utility Regulation; Federal Power Commission re Transcontinental Gas Pipe Line

Corporation; Michigan Public Service Commission re Michigan Gas and Electric Company.

5. We are discussing the deliberate choice of leverage with net operating earnings taken as given. Companies who find themselves at the limiting value of L are generally those who have suffered a decline in earnings since the original debt was issued, i.e., companies on the verge of, or in the process of reorganization or bankruptcy. One way of looking at the extreme range is to draw the k_o, k_e, and k_i curves rising rapidly for high values of leverage. This would imply that at 100 percent leverage k_o is well above the 10 percent level shown for zero leverage and V, well below \$1,000. However, at 100 percent leverage the bondholders are simply owners—with no senior securities ahead of them, i.e., the total value of the company cannot be below its hypothetical zero-leverage value of \$1,000 by more than the costs of reorganization. The question presents a difficult and interesting theoretical problem but not one of great practical significance. Presumably the way the k_o, k_e, and k_i curves behave at extreme limits of leverage will depend (a) on whether these limits are reached voluntarily, with no change in expected earnings, or involuntarily through reorganization, and (b) on the assumptions we wish to make about the willingness or unwillingness of prior creditors to hold new rights that are tantamount to ownership.

6. This is the general formulation for the cost of debt funds suggested by Durand. See "The Cost of Debt and Equity Funds for Business: Trends, Problems of Measurement," in Conference on Research in Business Finance, p. 225.

7. Durand, "The Cost of Debt and Equity Funds for Business: Trends, Problems of Measurement," in Conference on Research in Business Finance, pp. 229-30. See also Williams, The Theory of Investment Value, pp. 72-73; and Morton, "The Structure of the Capital Market and the Price of Money," American Economic Review, XLIV, 450-54.

8. Modigliani and Miller, "The Cost of Capital, Corporation Finance and the Theory of Investment," American Economic Review, XLVIII, 261-97.

9. The assumption that the yield curve is the same for all borrowers means that all borrowers with a given debt/equity ratio pay the same rate of interest. Since the rate on broker's loans to individuals has not been noticeably higher than over-all corporate borrowing rates, this assumption is not seriously out of line with general capital market conditions.

10. There has been some controversy about whether "arbitrage" is an appropriate name for the process or whether it should be referred to as "switching." See Durand, "The Cost of Capital, Corporation Finance

and the Theory of Investment: Comment," American Economic Review, XLIX, 639-54; and Modigliani and Miller, "The Cost of Capital, Corporation Finance, and the Theory of Investment: A Reply," American Economic Review, XLIX, 655-69.

    11. This is examined at length in the following chapter.

    12. Modigliani and Miller, "The Cost of Capital, Corporation Finance, and the Theory of Investment," American Economic Review, XLVIII, 274, no. 19.

IX. THE OPTIMAL USE OF LEVERAGE

One way of settling the issues raised by the startling differences between traditional beliefs and the Modigliani-Miller analysis is to "look at the evidence." Empirical studies have been made in order to isolate the effects of leverage—including two studies put forward by Modigliani and Miller in support of their position. However, even with the modern tools of statistical analysis, isolating the effect of one causal variable is a tricky task. It involves several difficulties, all of which are relevant in interpreting the results obtained from cross-sectional analysis of the data.

One major problem is that we must compare the individual capitalization rates of a reasonable number of companies which are homogeneous as far as business uncertainty is concerned but which differ fairly widely with respect to leverage or financial uncertainty. Such a group is hard to find. Groups which do have broadly similar business risks, e.g., electric utility companies, also tend to have broadly similar financial structures.

A second major problem is that what we must compare are capitalization rates, i.e., rates which equate future expected earnings to present market values. Such rates are of course not available and in their place it is necessary to use the ratio of current operating earnings or current net earnings to market value.[1]

Taken together, these difficulties mean that the regression equations uncovered for any sample of companies are subject to more than technically statistical errors. As Durand describes it:

"The influence, if any, of leverage on cost of capital has so far escaped detection in cross sections—both in the oils and utilities mentioned by MM, and in the bank stocks. But in view of the difficulties of empirical analysis, this is merely evidence of lack of evidence. On MM's scatter diagram (p. 283, Fig. 3), relating cost of capital to financial structure for 43 utilities in 1947-48, the ratio of "total earnings after taxes" to "market value of all securities" (i.e. cost of MM's definition) ranges roughly from $4\frac{1}{4}$ to $7\frac{1}{2}$ percent, with well over a third of the observations falling outside the range from 5 to $6\frac{1}{2}$ percent. In the face of so much scatter, could anyone be assured of detecting a consistent variation of, say, 1/4 percent? And a variation in capital cost of this magnitude would not be financially insignificant to a corporation manager or a public utilities commission. On assets of $1,000,000,000 savings of 1/4 percent would amount to the tidy sum of $2,500,000 per year. I submit that MM's apparently negative cross-section evidence is essentially inconclusive—especially when history provides positive evidence of periods like 1948-50, which were unusually favorable to bond financing, and others like 1958-59, which were unusually favorable to stock financing. The real significance of the lack of evidence in these cross-sections is to warn us that many important questions in corporation finance, the cost of capital, and the theory of investment are not easily answered with available data."[2]

But in spite of these limitations, the evidence does provide two significant findings. One is that the relation between the cost of capital and leverage for a given firm is clearly not a U-shaped function. Rather it appears to have a broad "horizontal" segment which covers a fairly wide range of leverage levels. Within this broad range observable changes in leverage seem to have virtually no effect on the overall cost of capital. In addition, the evidence confirms that increases in leverage, no matter how moderate, increase the equity capitalization rate k_e. Even if the evidence as a whole does not persuade traditionalists to abandon their entire position on leverage, these two specific findings deserve to be incorporated explicitly in any further restatements of the traditional view.

Empirical testing, in itself, is unlikely to provide a definitive resolution of the broader and more basic issue of whether an optimum range of leverage does or does not exist. The finding that the k_o curve derived from empirical studies is horizontal rather than U-shaped does not settle the basic issue. It is possible and defensible to argue that the majority of companies covered by the sample are operating within the optimal leverage range, in which k_o tends to be horizontal.

Thus the evidence that average observable values of k_o are probably horizontal with respect to observable variations in le-

verage can be interpreted in two ways. We can say with the traditionalists that this merely confirms that an optimal range of leverage does exist and that virtually all companies are sensible
enough to have found it. The implication of this interpretation is
that if companies move to leverage levels outside this range, their
over-all cost of capital will rise.

Alternatively we can say, with Modigliani and Miller, that the
evidence of horizontality over a reasonably wide range of leverage
levels confirms their theoretical proposition that the cost of capital is constant at all levels of leverage.

In short, the empirical findings are compatible with either
theory. Given the fact that a large enough number of observations
outside the horizontal range cannot be found, there appears to be
no conclusive way in which empirical tests of the kind already
done can settle the question of what is likely to happen to the cost
of capital at abnormally high levels of leverage. A resolution of
this question must depend on further analysis.

Further Analysis

In our earlier discussion we found it useful to separate the Modigliani-Miller proposition on leverage into two facets. One is
that increasing leverage, from zero up to some hypothetical point
we will refer to as acceptable, cannot raise total market value or
lower the cost of capital. The second is that increasing leverage
beyond the acceptable point cannot lower market value or raise the
cost of capital.

As Modigliani and Miller recognize, the first facet holds true
only if the effects of taxation and the tax deductibility of interest
charges are ignored. As we will see in the next chapter, increasing the use of debt funds can lower the cost of capital if taxes are
taken into account. Hence the real key to the controversy is the
validity of the second facet of their proposition, namely, that the
use of excessive leverage cannot impair total market value or
bring about an increase in the over-all cost of capital.

This conclusion holds if we assume that the rate of interest
paid on debt does not vary with leverage. At least it is possible,
given this assumption, to invoke the arbitrage argument in order
to show that it should hold if investors behave rationally.

However, we must lift the unrealistic assumption that the rate
of interest paid on debt does not vary with leverage. Instead we

will assume that it rises significantly as leverage is increased
beyond levels acceptable to the market, which includes lenders,
bond-rating agencies, and those who set investment and valuation
standards for the principal institutions supplying debt funds.

If we assume that k_i, the direct cost of debt capital, rises with
leverage, the Modigliani-Miller proposition that k_o remains constant has peculiar consequences for the equity-capitalization rate
k_e. For if k_i rises as leverage is increased beyond acceptable limits and k_o remains constant, then k_e must rise at a decreasing rate.
And as k_i continues to rise with increasing leverage, then k_e actually falls. The condition for a fall in k_e as leverage is increased
is given by $\Delta k_i > k_o$ where Δk_i is the marginal rate of interest paid
on additional borrowing, i.e., the change in total interest liabilities
divided by the extra amount of borrowing which brings about this
change.

It could be argued that no rational company will substitute debt
for equity if the marginal rate of interest on borrowing exceeds
the cost of pure equity capital, even when the effect that the extra
borrowing has on uncertainty is ignored. If this is accepted, then
for all practical purposes the argument between the traditional and
the Modigliani-Miller schools vanishes. Both would have to conclude that leverage is clearly excessive when the marginal rate of
interest exceeds k_e and that the use of leverage beyond this limit
lowers the market value of the company and raises its over-all
cost of capital.

However, Modigliani and Miller do not accept the fact that excessive leverage can ever cause the cost of capital function k_o to
turn upward. Their argument is that k_o remains constant with increasing leverage even if Δk_i exceeds k_e. This means that k_e falls
as leverage is increased in order to maintain k_o constant. In other
words, their hypothesis requires us to believe that k_e does fall,
i.e., that rational investors will value a more uncertain flow of
net earnings (in the more levered situation) more highly than they
value a less uncertain flow from the less levered situation.

As a specific illustration, let us assume that X and X* are two
identical companies in a given industry, except that X uses and
acceptable level of leverage and that X* uses a level higher than is
acceptable. Because of this, the average rate of interest, k_i^*, which
it pays is higher than the rate, k_i, paid by Company X. We will also
assume that both companies offer annual net operating earnings of
identical size and quality, and we will continue to ignore the effects
of taxation.

Let the value of X be $10,000, derived by capitalizing annual earnings of $1,000 at a rate k_o equal to 10 percent. Let B, the debt component of X, be $5,000. Then S, the value of the stock component, will also be $5,000. If k_i, the rate of interest paid by X, is 6 percent, k_e, its equity capitalization rate, will be 14 percent.

Now let X* have B* = $6,000, and because this is higher than the market finds acceptable, the rate of interest, k_i^* which the company has to pay on its debt is 8 percent. According to the Modigliani-Miller thesis, V*, the value of X*, cannot be anything other than $10,000 and its over-all cost of capital k_o^* must be 10 percent. Hence S*, the market value of stock, must be $4,000.[3] This means that its equity capitalization rate, k_e^*, is 13 percent. (Expected net operating earnings are $1,000 less $480 of interest on debt or net earnings of $520, which, relative to S* = $4,000, gives a rate $k_e^* = 13$ percent.)

Thus, according to the Modigliani-Miller hypothesis, k_c^* is less than k_e. In other words, the more uncertain flow of net earnings from the more heavily levered company X* is valued more highly than the less uncertain flow of net earnings from the less levered company X.

Modigliani and Miller recognize quite explicitly that their hypothesis implies that k_e falls as k_i rises when leverage is increased beyond acceptable limits.[4] What they do not recognize is that such a situation is completely incompatible with their own assumptions about rational investor behavior and perfect markets. It is difficult, and indeed impossible, to imagine why any rational group of investors would pay $4,000[5] for the overly-levered stock X* which offers net earnings of only $520 of relatively low quality when for the same price they could buy 80 percent of stock X and get net earnings of $560 of better quality.

The only explanation Modigliani and Miller offer in support of a k_e curve that falls as leverage is increased is as follows: "Should the demand by risk-lovers prove insufficient to keep the market to this peculiar yield-curve, this demand would be reinforced by the action of arbitrage operators."[6]

However, in this instance it is not at all clear, even within their restricted model, that what they call arbitrage will maintain the value of S* at $4,000 or k_e^* at 13 percent. A much better case can be made to show that rational investment behavior, including the process they call arbitrage, should force the value of S* below $4,000. In the first place, the existence of other investments, such as the stock of Company X, which offer a higher yield of higher

quality per dollar of investment, should lead rational investors to
sell X* stock and to purchase these other investments. But in addition to this, the arbitrage argument on which the Modigliani-
Miller argument depends can be used to show that persons holding X* stock will benefit by selling part of their holdings and
investing the proceeds plus some borrowed funds in the bonds of X*.
For example, a person who holds $1,000 worth of X* stock (i.e.,
one-fourth of the outstanding stock at the posited price of $4,000)
will benefit if he borrows $1,000 at 6 percent,[7] sells the stock, and
reinvests the $2,000 he now has in a package of bonds and stock in
company X*—with 60 percent or $1,200 in bonds and 40 percent or
$800 in stock.

With the original holding of X* stock alone he receives a one-
fourth share in the net operating earnings of X* or a pro rata claim
to net operating income of $250. But the company owes $480 in
interest to bondholders and his pro rata share in this liability is
$120. Thus he is left with net earnings of $130. After the partial
switch to bonds in the same company he will hold $800 in stock X*
or one-fifth of the total outstanding. Net operating earnings on
this will be $200. His pro rata share of interest payable by the
company is $96. But now as a bondholder as well he receives in-
terest from the company on $1,200 of bond holdings. This is also
$96. These two items, his share as a stockholder of the company
interest payable on bonds and his receipt as a bondholder of company interest paid on bonds, are identical in size and quality and
therefore cancel out. This leaves him with net operating earnings
of $200. On this he pays personal interest on his $1,000 loan from
his bank or broker, which at 6 percent amounts to $60—leaving
net earnings after interest of $140. This is higher than the $130
he would have had on his original holding of stock, and furthermore, it involves less financial uncertainty. Thus, according to
Modigliani and Miller's own prescription for rational behavior,
investors holding Stock X* have a strong incentive to sell part of
their holdings in favor of bonds if the total price of the stock is
$4,000. This selling pressure will push the price of stock to some
point below $4,000.

Assuming that the price of X* bonds is fixed by investment attitudes of the bond market (i.e., that the effective yield on these
bonds is purely a function of leverage and remains at 8 percent),
then the argument given above must mean that the stock of Company X* will keep declining until the opportunity for gain through

arbitrage is erased. This will happen when S* falls to $3,408.50
(ignoring brokerage and transfer fees). At S* = $3,408.50, stock-
holders in X* no longer have an incentive to sell part of their holdings in order to buy bonds in Company X*. At S* = $3,408.50, the
expected yield on stock alone is 15.256 percent: the expected yield
on a mixture of stocks and bonds in the same company, after payment of personal interest on borrowed funds is also 15.256 percent.

At S* = $3,408.50, the highly levered stock of Company X* with
k_s^* = 15.256 percent is also more in line with other stocks available in the market such as Company X stock, which has less leverage but also offers a lower return—in this case, 14 percent. Indeed it is possible to argue that the yield spread between the
shares X and X* may now be higher than is justified by their difference in financial uncertainty and that holders of X stock may
want to switch to X*. There is no way in which yield spreads and
risk differences can be directly equated, but we can use the arbitrage device as a crude and indirect check on whether or not S =
$5,000 and S* = $3,408.50 are in mutual equilibrium. In this case
it turns out that the value at which X* stock reaches equilibrium
with X* bonds, i.e., S* = 3,408.50 is not in equilibrium with the
value of a rival stock, S = $5,000. Holders of X can gain by selling
their holdings, borrowing on personal account, and then reinvesting in a mixture of stocks and bonds of Company X*. (The proportions of bonds to stock to be bought are identical to the bond-stock
proportions in X*'s capital structure.) Thus a one-fifth owner of
X obtains net operating earnings from his holding equal to $200,
on which the company pays interest equal to $60, leaving net earn-
ings of $140. By selling this holding for $1,000, borrowing $882
at 6 percent, and investing $1,200 in bonds of X* and $682 in X*
stock, he can increase his expected yield. The new holdings will
give him the same net operating earnings as before, i.e., he will
now be holding one-fifth of Company X*. His share in the company's liability for interest on its bonds is $96 (one-fifth of $480)
but this is exactly offset by his $96 share in bond-interest paid by
the company ($1,200 at 8 percent). This leaves him with net oper-
ating earnings in X* of $200. From this he pays his personal in-
terest of $53 on his broker's loan of $882, leaving him with a net
yield of $147. This is better than he could have expected from his
original holding in X.

We can infer from this kind of arbitrage analysis (and this may well turn out to be the most important use of Modigliani and Miller's arbitrage device) that at k_e = 14 percent and k_e^* = 15.256, the difference in relative yields is out of line with the leverage-induced differences in financial uncertainty between the two stocks. This disequilibrium will induce "rational" investors to switch from X to X* and this will bring about price changes in either or both until equilibrium is restored. Since our earlier assumption that the yield on X* bonds is rigidly fixed at 8 percent, this fixes the stock yield of X* stock at 15.256 and we are forced to assume that equilibrium will be restored through a fall in the price of X stock and a rise in its yield to some rate higher than 14 percent. Based entirely on a literal and mechanistic application of the arbitrage line of argument, the new equilibrium yield for X will be k_e = 14.88 percent, at which S = \$4,704.[8] At S = \$4,704, S* = \$3,408.50, k_e = 14.88 percent, k_e^* = 15.256 percent, k_i = 6 percent, and k_i^* = 8 percent, with all other factors taken as given and fixed (such as net operating earnings), we have a situation in which all the securities involved are in equilibrium.

The market value V of the moderately or wisely levered Company X will be \$5,000 (of bonds) plus \$4,704 of stock, or a total of \$9,704. Its overall cost of capital k_o is 10.30 percent. (Given by the ratio of net operating earnings of \$1,000 to \$9,704.)

The value V_o^* of the heavily or overly-levered Company X* will be \$6,000 of bonds plus \$3,408 of stock, or a total of \$9,408. Its overall cost of capital k_o^* is 10.62 percent. (Given by the ratio of net operating earnings of \$1,000 to \$9,408.)

Taken together, the two sets of values indicate that the use of leverage beyond the point acceptable to creditors can lower total market value and raise a company's cost of capital above what it would be if leverage were used more judiciously. In short, given that creditors have certain attitudes toward the safe amount of debt borrowers should be allowed to carry, there is a limiting debt/equity ratio for a company, above which the cost of capital rises with further increases in leverage.

The Effect of Taxation

Finally, we must expand the analysis to introduce the effect of corporate income taxes, and particularly the effect of the tax-deductibility of interest charges.[9]

The fact that interest payments are deductible before a corporation's tax liabilities are computed increases the rate of after-tax net earnings for a levered corporation relative to an unlevered one. For example, if we take two otherwise identical companies, X and X*, each of which offers net operating earnings of $1,000 of like quality, and assume that X is debt-free whereas X* has $3,000 of debt at 4 percent, the total market value of X will be larger than the total market value of X*, even if we assume that the returns are capitalized at identical rates. At an average corporate income tax rate of 50 percent we would have:

	X	X*
Net operating earnings	$ 1,000	$ 1,000
Interest	0	$ 120
Net earnings	$ 1,000	$ 880
Taxes (at 50 percent)	$ 500	$ 440
Net earnings after tax	$ 500	$ 440
Total returns to security holders after tax[10]	$ 500	$ 560
After-tax capitalization rate	x_o = .05	
Total value of company V	$10,000	$11,200
Value of bonds B	0	$ 3,000
Value of stock S	$10,000	$ 8,200
After-tax equity capitalization rate x_e	.05	.05365

The higher value of Company X* is not due to the valuation approach used but to the gain derived from lower tax liabilities relative to the unlevered company. The data in the illustration use the net operating earnings approach to valuation which is the one used by Modigliani and Miller. The only modification is that the over-all capitalization rate is independent of leverage, only so long as leverage is within "acceptable limits."

Since we are now discussing returns net of corporate income taxes, the relevant capitalization rate is the after-tax capitalization rate which we denote by x_o to distinguish it from k_o, the before-tax rate. Even though x_o is the same for both companies, reflecting the fact that the degree of uncertainty is the same for both, total market value is higher for the levered company because its use of debt makes its tax liability smaller. Because of the tax factor, increased leverage (within acceptable limits) increases total market value.

A company's over-all cost of capital on a before-tax basis,

i.e., the minimum before-tax rate of return required on new investments, is still given by k_o, the rate which relates net operating earnings before interest and taxes to total market value. But since market value varies with leverage, k_o also varies with leverage. Thus, in the example, Company X has a cost of capital of 10 percent, whereas for Company X* the cost is 8.928 percent (given by the ratio of $1,000 to $11,200). The influence of leverage on k_o depends on three factors: (1) the tax rate to (2) the degree of leverage used measured as B/V and (3) k_i, the average rate of interest paid on debt.

We have

$$k_o = \frac{x_o - tk_i(B/V)}{1 - t}$$ (9.1)[11]

where x_o is the over-all after-tax capitalization rate, which is a function of the business uncertainty involved and is a constant for all companies in a given risk class. The effect of the tax-deductibility of interest is that k_o declines with leverage. For an all-equity company the cost of capital is simply $x_o/(1 - t)$, or in the example (which assumes a flat 50 percent tax rate) this is $.05/.5$, or $.10$. As leverage is increased k_o declines, and the amount of decline is equal to $tk_i(B/V)/(1 - t)$. In our own illustration this is $.04\ B/V$. Thus Company X*, with leverage of $B/V = 3,000/11,200$, enjoys a decline in its cost of capital of 1.072 percent relative to the unlevered Company X.

We get exactly the same results if we measure the cost of capital in terms of the alternative formulations put forward in chapter VI. Thus we can measure k_o as a weighted average cost of capital. This formulation would give:

$$k_o = \frac{x_e(S/V) + k_i(i - t)(B/V)}{1 - t}$$ (9.2)

where x_e is the after-tax equity capitalization rate. In the example, we would again have $k_o = 8.928$ percent for the levered Company X* and k_o would again be a function of leverage.

Finally, we could set our financial standards in terms of the minimum required rate of return on equity investment. In this formulation we would require the investment to yield a minimum return, after interest and taxes, equal to x_e, the after-tax equity capitalization rate, and we would have:

$$k_o = \frac{x_e \cdot (S/V) + k_i (B/V)}{1 - t} \qquad (9.3)$$

Whatever formulation we choose to use, the tax advantage of using debt, in itself, reduces a company's cost of capital as leverage is increased.[12]

Conclusions

To return to our basic thesis, we can now combine the two arguments we have presented on the relation between leverage and the cost of capital. Whether in a tax-free world the traditional view about k_o is correct, or whether the Modigliani-Miller argument that k_o does not fall with leverage is correct, in a world of taxable incomes and the deductibility of interest there can be little doubt that k_o falls as leverage is increased.

However, the fall in k_o does not go on through all ranges of leverage. Beyond debt limits acceptable to lenders the tax benefits from still more leverage are first offset and then later more than offset by accompanying rises in k_i and k_e.

In short, the cost of capital function has a shape very like that postulated in the traditional literature and described earlier, although the reasons for this are not exactly those envisaged by the traditional point of view. For moderate degrees of leverage (moderate with respect to capital market standards), the use of debt lowers a company's cost of capital. As leverage is increased, the tax benefits from debt are approximately offset by a rise both in k_i and k_e and the overall cost of capital changes little, i.e., it has a horizontal segment, up to the point where the marginal rate of interest approaches the equity capitalization rate. Beyond this point, creditors are unlikely to permit further increases in leverage, but any company which insists on increasing its use of debt is likely to find that its cost of capital rises. There is an optimal range of leverage as far as the cost of capital consideration is concerned and at the upper end it is bounded by the point of leverage beyond which the marginal rate of interest demanded by the market exceeds the average cost of capital at that point. The location of this point is largely a function of standards held by lending institutions and is based on their evaluation of the business risks which the enterprise faces.

NOTES

1. One by-product of the empirical tests of the leverage effect is that the debate on leverage has been broadened to include the related question of whether dividend payout ratios should not be included as an independent determinant of market values and hence of capitalization rates. See Lintner, "A New Model of the Cost of Capital: Dividends, Earnings, Leverage, Expectations and Stock Prices"; and Modigliani and Miller, "Leverage, Dividend Policy and the Cost of Capital" (unpublished papers presented at the annual meeting of the Econometric Society, December, 1960, St. Louis, Missouri).

2. Durand, "The Cost of Capital, Corporation Finance, and the Theory of Investment: Comment," American Economic Review, XLIX, 652-53. "MM" refers to Modigliani and Miller.

3. Actually, if we assume that a substantial part of X*'s debt was issued earlier at some rate lower than 8 percent, then B* will be less than $6,000 and this would make S* higher than $4,000. We will ignore this refinement although its use would add to the case being made.

4. Modigliani and Miller, "The Cost of Capital, Corporation Finance, and the Theory of Investment," American Economic Review, XLVIII, 275.

5. To keep the arithmetic at the simplest level, the illustration deals with the whole $4,000 rather than part of it.

6. Modigliani and Miller, "The Cost of Capital, Corporation Finance, and the Theory of Investment," American Economic Review, XLVIII, 276. It is interesting to note that in this case the authors introduce subjective risk preferences as a possible determinant of values, i.e., they suggest that investors may be willing to pay a premium for more uncertainty and that market value may reflect this willingness. But if we assume the same thing for phases of moderate leverage, we are led directly to the conclusions reached by traditional theory, namely, that small increases in leverage (which do not increase k_1) can increase total market value and lower the over-all cost of capital!

7. We are assuming, with Modigliani and Miller, that persons pay the same rate as companies. In this example, the relevant rate for a 50 percent margin loan will be 6 percent, the rate paid by Company X.

8. At S = $4,740, the net yield on a package of X* bonds and stocks after personal interest is exactly equal in size and quality to the net yield on X stock.

9. Tax deductibility of interest charges is not the only route through which tax structure may have an influence on financial structure, although it is probably the most important route, especially when excess profits taxes are in effect. Closely held corporations may prefer debt to equity

for other reasons as well. For example, property valuations are more likely to be accepted by control authorities if the transfer to a company is in exchange for debt rather than equity securities. Also, in the event of losses, debt can be written off as ordinary losses under the personal income tax rather than as capital losses. Finally, if the corporation accumulates value by using retained earnings to pay off debt, this is less likely to be regarded as a tax-avoiding device under the "unreasonable accumulation of surplus" clause (Sections 531-37, Internal Revenue Code of 1954). Furthermore, if the debt holders also happen to be family members, there is the advantage that the proceeds received from debt retirement can be counted for their personal income tax purposes as a tax free return of capital rather than as a regular dividend. On the other hand, it must also be remembered that the lower capital gains tax on retained earnings does to some extent offset the tax advantage of debt as opposed to internal equity financing.

10. Equal to net earnings after tax plus interest.

11. This ignores the slight element of progression in the corporate income tax. From the numerical example given earlier we can see that the over-all after-tax capitalization rate is

$$x_o = \frac{(O - k_i B)(1 - t) + k_i B}{V}$$

from which we get

$$\frac{O}{V}(i - t) = x_o + \frac{(k_i B)}{V} - \frac{(k_i B)}{V} - k_i t \cdot \frac{B}{V}$$

Since $k_o = \frac{O}{V}$, we have the result shown in eq. (9.1).

12. The easiest way to see that the formulation given in eqs. (9.1), (9.2), and (9.3) gives identical results is to examine all three in terms of the numerical illustration.

X. INVESTMENT DECISIONS

The last chapter substantially completes our survey of the theoretical backdrop to investment and financing decisions. We turn, in this chapter and the next, to some of the problems and techniques associated with the decisional process itself.

Ongoing Investments

A logical point of departure both for investment decisions and financing decisions is a continuing analysis of how ongoing operations are performing. The central framework conventionally used for this purpose, and one which lends itself to most of the major facets of financial management such as planning, budgeting, coordination, evaluation, and control, is summarized below in Figure 5. The kind of analysis implied by this outline can be conducted by product lines or by divisions, and comparisons can be made either against corresponding company data for past periods or against norms developed on the basis of industry-wide experience. The data themselves are by-products of normal accounting processes, but the arrangement provides a convenient framework for a quick review of emerging trends, an over-all focus of control, and a point of departure for subsequent and more detailed diagnosis and analysis of specific decisional problems.[1] All three facets of the conventional analysis are relevant for investment and financing decisions.

1. When combined with a forecast of sales and revenues, a detailed analysis of past and current trends provides the basis for operating and cash-flow budgets for the period ahead, generally one year. This gives an estimate of the amount of funds that operations are expected to generate, of the required commitment of

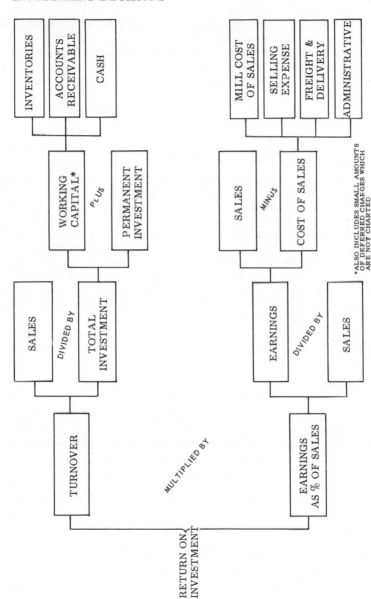

Fig. 5. Relationship of Factors Affecting Return on Investment

funds for increased working capital, and hence of the gross amount of financing available from operations.[2]

2. It provides a basis for "controlling" investment in the various forms of assets used in ongoing operations and a preliminary test of whether asset usage is being managed effectively. While the various ratios that can be drawn from the overall framework are not a satisfactory basis for evaluating management performance as such, they serve remarkably well as a device for isolating those operations in which asset-usage is not producing commensurate returns.[3] This in turn may lead to investment or disinvestment decisions.

3. Finally, the information derived from the analysis influences the capital expenditure and financing budget in several ways. It is a basis for estimating the size and quality of future returns from existing operations—which in turn is the basis for estimating a company's cost of capital or its cutoff point for new capital expenditures. It also influences top management's own evaluation of estimates submitted in connection with new investment proposals. Finally, wherever the initial diagnosis leads to further analysis and to reinvestment or abandonment decisions, the associated commitment or release of funds or facilities becomes part of the capital budget for the coming period.

With this very brief review of the problems of ongoing investment, we will turn to the problem of the capital expenditure budget and the analysis of porposed new investments.[4]

Measuring the Profitability of New Investments

Business firms have always faced the problem of evaluating the profitability of new investments in assets. The methods used have ranged from highly subjective-intuitive-judgmental approaches to objective-quantified approaches. The difference is one of degree rather than of kind: all evaluation of the future requires subjective judgment and even a measure of intuition. But at one extreme the necessary insights are translated directly into decisions; at the other they are first developed into explicit estimates of expected revenues, costs, and benefits, which are next transformed into measures of profitability that in turn form the basis for decisions.

The general trend in capital expenditure management has been toward the objective approach. One result of this trend is that the problem of converting estimates of costs and benefits into a reli-

able yardstick of investment worth has received increasing attention—and a very large literature has blossomed on this subject
during the past ten years.[5]

Apart from subjective-qualitative yardsticks, there are four
basic approaches to the measurement of investment worth. These
are:

1. Payback period.
2. Book return on book investment.
3. Internal rate of return.
4. Contribution to net present worth.

Payback period. This is simply the ratio obtained by dividing
the original depreciable fixed investment in an asset by gross annual profit expected before any allowance for depreciation. It
measures the number of years required for the gross earnings on
the project (with no allowance for capital wastage) to pay back the
original outlay. Also known as the payoff period or the cash recovery period, this is probably the most widely used quantitative
measure of investment worth. The most obvious defect of the payback period is that it does not measure profitability. In other
words it ignores what happens after a project has returned its investment.

Attempts have been made to salvage the concept as a measure
of profitability by adjusting the concept itself, and many such variants have been advocated, all under the same name. For example,
the payback period has been computed as the ratio of investment
to net earnings after an allowance for depreciation, or to average
net earnings after an allowance for depreciation. This variant, or
its reciprocal, is very similar to the yardstick provided by the
second broad approach to the management of profitability, book
return on book investment.

The payback period in its original and proper sense is a time
concept, not a rate concept, and it is convenient to confine the term
to its original meaning, namely, the estimated period required for
incremental cash investments in a project to be recovered from
year-to-year incremental throw-off of cash (after taxes, but before depreciation) attributable to a project.

In this form it does provide a coarse screening device which
will pick off high-profit projects that are so clearly desirable as
to require no refined estimates of profitability, or to reject quickly
those proposals that show such poor promise that they do not warrant further analysis. It is also a useful measure when liquidity,

as opposed to profitability, is a dominant short-run consideration, for example, in the rare case of companies which have a high volume of internal investment opportunities but relatively low access to internal or external sources of funds.

The trouble with the payback yardstick is not the concept itself but the way it is used. It tends to be used illogically for purposes outside its scope, either as an index of profitability or as a basis for ranking relative merit of rival proposals, or finally, in the form of a maximum acceptable payback period as a standard of required performance. In these uses it can often be dangerously deceptive. While most managements are fully aware of these limitations and hazards, it is clear from the many variant forms of payback which have been developed that there is a perennial temptation to stretch the use of a simple measure like payback to tasks outside its inherent scope.

If payback is to be extended so that it provides a generally applicable measure of investment worth, it is necessary to measure not only the payback period, but the size and duration of returns expected beyond this period. Whenever the after-payback duration is long, the reciprocal of the payback becomes a good approximation of true profitability. If the post-payback duration is zero, the true rate of return is also zero, and the project is worthless no matter how short the payback period itself is. However, the task of keeping one eye on payback and another on post-payback duration is awkward, and since the two dimensions have to be integrated into a single judgment anyway, it is far more satisfactory to do so explicitly. But when this is done, the original concept of payback period vanishes and we are left with one variant or another of a computed rate of return.[6]

Book Return on Book Investment. Also known as the accounting method, level book rate-of-return method, or average book method or simply as return on investment, this method of figuring profitability takes the ratio of average annual profits expected from the project (conventionally computed) to book investment in the project.

The method has a host of variants: indeed, one of its shortcomings is that it is an altogether ambiguous concept, particularly with respect to the computation of the denominator of the ratio. Original book investment is sometimes used, sometimes, average book investment, sometimes, a weighted average of period-by-period book investment. It is also ambiguous with respect to the concept of investment itself. In a strict sense, being a book-value measure, it should include only capitalized outlays, including working capital required, but this is frequently broadened to include all expected outlays connected with a project.

Apart from the ambiguities involved the method fails to take into account the timing of expected earnings or of expected outlays. It therefore provides a correct measure of the rate of return only under fairly specific conditions, i.e., when outlays "occur" at a single point of time, when expected benefits do flow evenly over the life of the project, and where economic life corresponds to the life assumed for bookkeeping purposes. Without these conditions the results derived from this approach or from this set of approaches are subject to fairly wide errors.[7]

The Internal Rate of Return. The internal rate of return is the true rate at which an investment is repaid by proceeds from a project. In operational terms, it is that rate at which the incremental cash benefits expected from a project (after taxes, but before an allowance for depreciation) have a discounted present value which is exactly equal to the discounted present value of all incremental outlays required for the project's implementation.

It is conceptually identical to the method, long used by the financial world, for computing the expected yield to maturity of a bond which is purchased for an amount different from its face value. Thus it has also been called the true-yield method, or the investor's method.[8] Other names given to it are the discounted cash-flow method,[9] the interest-rate-of-return,[10] and the scientific method.[11] Economic theory has generally referred to it as the internal rate of return[12] or the marginal efficiency of capital.[13]

Numerical illustrations provide the most explicit way of understanding the nature of the internal rate of return, and the difference between it and the two earlier measures of profitability.

To begin with the simplest kind of example, take a 5 percent $1,000 bond, which can be purchased at $1,000 which offers interest at the rate of $50 per annum, and which will mature in exactly 5 years. The intuitive answer for the question of rate of return on this bond is 5 percent per annum—and this is the answer we get from any approach we use. But why is it 5 percent? Because the coupon rate is 5 percent? Obviously not. Because the ratio of annual interest to outlay is 5 percent? Many people might say yes. Because 5 percent is the reciprocal of its payback period (20 years if its impending maturity date is ignored)? Some would agree.

The actual reason that 5 percent happens to be the correct answer is strange, unfamiliar, and lengthy: the rate of return is exactly 5 percent per annum because only at 5 percent is the time-adjusted value of expected net receipts equal to the time-adjusted value of net outlays. In other words, because k = .05 is the only value which satisfies the equation:[14]

$$1,000 = \frac{50}{1 + k} + \frac{50}{(1 + k)^2} + \cdots \frac{50}{(1 + k)^5} + \frac{1,000}{(1 + k)^5}$$

For one, two, and three time periods, k can be solved for explicitly. As the number of time periods in the equation increases, explicit solutions become increasingly difficult and finally impossible and k must be found by a process of trial and error, i.e., we look up the value of the right-hand side of the equation for various values of k and select that which satisfies the equation. In the equation given, the "correct" method seems like and unnecessarily complex approach to a simple problem. But when the problem is replaced by one just a little less simple, the "correct" approach actually becomes the shortest route to an acceptable solution for the rate of return promised by a proposal.

For example, let us amend the illustration we have so that the net purchase price of the bond is not $1,000 but $1,044.52. Now most of the simple answers are clearly wrong. The rate is no longer equal to the coupon rate of 5 percent. Nor is it equal to 4.786 percent, the reciprocal of the hypothetical payback period. And it is equally wrong to say that it can be found by dividing 50 by $1,044.52—which also gives 4.786, the same answer as the reciprocal of the payback period—because this ignores the capital loss of $44.52 the investor suffers when he redeems the bond for less than its purchase price.

We can proceed to amend the simple approach to take complications into account. For example we can allow for a recovery of the $44.52 of expected depreciation in five equal annual instalments by subtracting $8.90 from each year's gross interest receipt, i.e., we compute on the basis of a net income of $41.10 and divide this net figure by $1,044.52. This gives 3.935 percent, a very different answer than we had before but still a wrong answer. This time the error is due to the fact that we do not have $1,044.52 invested for 5 years: rather our investment declines by the annual recovery of the depreciation allowance of $8.90. One way out of this problem is to take average investment rather than initial investment as the

denominator. Now we have $41.10 divided by $1,022.26, 4.021 percent for our answer. And still further refinements are possible,
such as some allowance for the fact that $1,022.26 is not an exact
measure of the average capital tie-up, i.e., we could take a
weighted average: $1,044.52 for 5 years, $1,035.62 for 4 years,
and so on.

In short, the simple approaches turn out to be not so simple
after all. In contrast, the apparently more "complex" approach
provides a single straightforward answer which is unambiguous
and correct. In this case there is one rate and only one rate which
equates the present value of the receipts to the present value of
outlays and this rate is exactly 4 percent. This is not remarkably
different from the answers provided by the adjusted book-value
approaches, only because the problem itself is still a very simple
one. In more complex investment situations, in which outlays take
place over several periods of time and in which expected receipts
do not flow in equal annual instalments, the various methods may
produce answers that differ very widely from the correct one.

That the answer provided by the internal rate of return is actually correct can be seen by examining any given situation in reverse. For example, assume that $1,044.52 is invested in a bank
at a rate of 4 percent per annum, that $50 a year is withdrawn
each year beginning 12 months after the deposit and, finally, that
$1,000 is withdrawn after exactly 5 years. Assuming there are no
bank charges the account will show a zero balance at the end of
five years, as follows:

Year	Interest (in dollars)	Withdrawal (in dollars)	Net Balance (in dollars)
0	–	–	1,044.52
1	41.78	50	1,036.30
2	41.45	50	1,027.75
3	41.11	50	1,018.86
4	40.75	50	1,009.62
5	40.38	50	1,000.00
–	–	1,000	0

The bond investment and the bank investment offer identical
cash flows. Since we know that the rate of return at the bank is 4
percent it must follow that the correct answer for the yield on the
bond is also 4 percent. Methods that give a different answer are
therefore incorrect.

<u>Objections to the Internal Rate of Return.</u> Several features of
the internal rate of return as a practical measure of profitability
cause perennial concern among businessmen. It seems to arrive
at its result by a direct comparison of gross cash flows, and in
this process depreciation and capital wastage are ignored. In fact,
depreciation is not ignored. Book depreciation is relevant for purposes of computing tax liabilities and incremental tax liabilities
attributable to a project are computed on a conventional basis,
after normal allowance for depreciation. But although taxes are
deducted, the annual allowance for depreciation itself is not sub-
tracted from the receipts side of the equation. Indeed, the method
makes no attempt to separate return of investment from return on
investment. Instead it treats all returns as returns to investment:
but the fact that estimated salvage values for most business investments are a lot lower than original outlays does enter the
equation explicitly and in this sense true expected depreciation is
fully taken into account. The period-by-period segregation of true
income from capital recovery is an important aspect of accounting
for purposes of tax and financial reporting, but it is unnecessary
for the task of computing the annual rate of return promised by a
proposal over its expected economic life.

A second source of misgiving exists in situations where outlays take place over several periods. Take, for example, an outlay of $20 now, followed by a subsequent outlay of $10 a year,
which offers to yield a gross return (including recovery of capital) of $35.20 two years hence. The internal rate of return on such
a proposal is 10 percent. That this is a "correct" rate can be
tested by assuming that one invests corresponding amounts in a
bank at 10 percent. But the process of computing the internal rate
of return is to discount the expected cash flows in order to find
that rate at which net present value is zero. Doing this seems to
suggest that the first outlays of $20 actually "earns" 10 percent
between its investment date and one year later, whereas in fact
it yields nothing during this period. The answer is that the internal rate of return is an average annual concept which measures
the average rate of yield over the entire life of the project.

A third apparently troublesome feature of the internal rate of
return is that it requires cash flow estimates which are difficult,
and sometimes impossible, to obtain. This misgiving confuses
the estimating problem with the computational problem. All measures of profitability require correct estimates if they are to yield
correct answers. All that the internal rate approach does is to in-

sist that the timing of cash flows is a relevant consideration—which it is. If there is evidence that these flows do not occur at an equal annual pace, this factor must be taken into account in assaying investment worth. If there is no evidence on this, the usual solution is to treat expected receipts as if they will flow evenly. But this also implies a forecast about timing. The question of getting the estimates is one issue. How the best available estimates are translated into a single overall measure of profitability is a separate issue. Given estimates of a certain quality, the internal rate method is the only correct way of translating them into such a measure.

Indeed, the more difficult the estimating problem the more it pays to use the internal rate approach. For example, where the economic life of a project and the size of distant receipts are both highly uncertain, the average book measure, which is affected equally by distant inflows and by immediate future inflows, is far more likely to yield misleading results. In contrast, the computational process of the internal rate automatically handicaps the more distant expectations (and at rates relevant to business investment this handicapping effect is very large), and thus minimizes the effect of the errors to which distant estimates are subject.

Finally, the computational problem itself is a source of concern. Businessmen who do not hesitate to look up a mortgage interest table when they buy a home somehow balk at the idea of consulting a compound interest table to find the rate offered on an internal investment. In practice the actual clerical work involved is relatively trivial and can be handled with less skill than it requires to manipulate a typewriter or fill in a personal income-tax return.

There is a second type of possible misunderstanding, at an altogether different level, regarding the computational question. This is the discovery, or rediscovery, of the fact that certain patterns of benefits and outlays cannot be expressed in terms of a single, unique rate of return. In these situations, the literal application of the usual prescription for finding the internal rate of return, i.e., to find that rate of discount which equates net incremental benefits to net incremental outlays required, may yield not just one but two or more solutions for the rate of return implied by an investment proposal.[15]

For example, assume that the proposal being considered is the installation of a larger oil pump that would get a fixed quantity of oil out of the ground more rapidly than the pump that is already in use. Let us assume that, by operating the existing pump, the investor can expect $10,000 a year hence and $10,000 two years hence. Let us assume that by installing the larger pump at a net cost of $1,600 now he can expect $20,000 a year hence and nothing the second year. The installation of the larger pump can be viewed as a project having the cash flow characteristics shown below.

Time Period	Incremental Cash Flow Due to Investment (in dollars)
t_0	− 1,600
t_1	+10,000
t_2	−10,000

The usual prescription for finding the rate of return of a project is to find that rate which makes the discounted value of net cash flows equal to the discounted value of capital outlays. Alternatively, and this amounts to the same thing, find that rate which makes the algebraic sum of the discounted cash outflows and inflows equal to zero. The application of this method to our example will yield two answers, 25 and 400 percent. In other words, using a 25 percent rate, the discounted value of the cash flows is exactly equal to the outlay of $1,600. However, a rate of 400 percent also equates cash flows with capital outlay. Which of the two rates is the correct measure of the investment worth of the project, 25 or 400 percent?

Neither of these rates is a measure of investment worth, neither has relevance to the profitability of the project under consideration, and neither, therefore, is correct. The fault lies in the incorrect application of the "usual prescription" for finding the rate of return.

The correct solution for the investment worth of the project is simple. But it requires an explicit answer to a relevant question: "What is it worth to the investor to receive $10,000 one year earlier than he would have otherwise received it?" This is actually all that the installation of the larger pump achieves. If the investor expects to be able to put the $10,000 to work at a yield of x percent per annum, then getting the money a year earlier is worth $100x. If x is 23 percent, for example, getting $10,000 a year earlier is worth $2,300. In other words, if he spent $1,600 on the larger pump now (at time t_0), he would end up at time t_2 having $2,300 more than he otherwise would have had. This can be stated as an equivalent "rate of return," which in this case would be about 20 percent ($1,600 at 20 percent per annum would amount to $2,304 at the end of two years). Using this approach, a unique and meaningful rate of return can always be found for any set of cash inflows and outflows.

Relevant Costs, Revenues, and Tables

The heart of the investment evaluation problem is not computational methodology but estimation. The existence of a precise computational methodology does, however, force management to make explicit estimates that otherwise might be made only implicitly. But it requires no estimates that a good decision would not require anyway.

Whatever the method used, the concepts being estimated for the purpose of evaluating a new investment require careful definition. The relevant outlays to be taken into account in assaying a proposal are incremental outlays, i.e., total expected outlays, if the proposal is instituted, less total outlays expected in the absence of the proposal. These include items generally carried on the books as capital as well as other outlays that may never show on the balance sheet. Similarly, continuing costs attributed to a proposal may contain items generally thought of as "prime" or "direct" or "variable," but they may also contain items generally thought of as "overhead." In either case the central concept is one of incremental costs or outlays. The same is true of the receipt side of the equation.

The only conceptual problem where some ambiguity exists relates to the kind of compound interest or compound discount table to be used. The values contained in any given interest or discount table depend on the frequency of compounding assumed. At 10 percent the compound amount of one dollar at the end of one year is $1.10 on an annual compounding basis. If interest is compounded semiannually it is $1.1025. With quarterly compounding it is $1.1038. The amount rises with the frequency of compounding till at the limit, with an infinitely small compounding interval and infinitely frequent, instantaneous, or continuous compounding, it is $1.1052.

Obviously, present values, which are simply reciprocals of compound amounts, also differ with the frequency of compounding assumed. Which table of present values should be used in computing the rate of return on investment, the annual basis, a quarterly basis, or continuous compounding? Many of the major financial outflows from a business take place at discrete intervals but these intervals vary from item to item. For example, taxes and dividends are generally paid quarterly, interest is paid semiannually, salaries monthly, and so on. But many of the inflows occur more or less continuously. Given this fact, no particular compounding interval is exactly appropriate.

The problem is of theoretical rather than practical significance. The difference between results obtained from using an annual compounding interval as against continuous compounding is small. These differences for a sample of rates and time periods, are shown in Table 2. At low rates of interest and for short spans of time, the differences are negligible. As rates and time spans become higher, the relative difference in present values becomes significant. But because the present values of distant sums falls very sharply at high rates of discount, the absolute difference in final results obtained in solving for the rate of returns is minor.

Rate of Return Versus Present Worth

Computing a project's internal rate of return is one step in the measurement of investment worth. The second step is to compare this rate RR against the company's cost of capital k. If RR is larger than k, the proposal should be accepted; if RR is less than k, it should be rejected.[16]

An alternative approach, which we listed earlier as the fourth method of measuring investment worth, is to compute the algebraic sum of the present value of expected outlays attributable to a project, and the present value of incremental benefits, with both streams discounted at the rate k. If the net present worth is positive the proposal should be accepted; if negative, it should be rejected.

Both approaches yield identical results as far as "accept or reject" decisions are concerned. This is so because the net present worth of a project is greater than, equal to, or less than zero if, as, and when the RR is greater than, equal to, or less than k. Thus, both provide a universally correct yardstick for determining the worth of an individual investment outlay.

However, for the purpose of ranking and hence selecting from among two or more alternative proposals which are mutually exclusive, the two approaches may yield contradictory results. The relative ranking problem is a common one. For example, two pro-

Table 2. Difference Between Continuous (C) and Annual (A) Discounting Intervals Present Value of One Dollar Due at the End of N Years

N	5 percent		10 percent		15 percent		20 percent	
	C	A	C	A	C	A	C	A
1	.9512	.9524	.9048	.9091	.8607	.8696	.8187	.8333
5	.7788	.7835	.6065	.6209	.4724	.4972	.3679	.4019
10	.6065	.6139	.3679	.3855	.2231	.2472	.1353	.1615
15	.4724	.4810	.2231	.2394	.1054	.1229	.0498	.0649
20	.3679	.3769	.1353	.1486	.0498	.0611	.0183	.0261
25	.2865	.2953	.0821	.0923	.0235	.0304	.0067	.0105

Source: Ezra Solomon, ed., The Management of Corporate Capital (Glencoe, Illinois: The Free Press), p. 321

posals may represent alternative ways of doing the same thing; both are good in an absolute sense, but since only one can be undertaken the relevant question is which is better.

Let us use the following illustration. Assume a company has two mutually exclusive proposals, A and B, each involving an outlay of $2,225 now and offering the following net cash inflows:

Year	Project A (in dollars)	Project B (in dollars)
0	− 2,225	− 2,225
1	1,000	0
2	1,000	500
3	1,000	1,000
4	1,000	3,343
5	0	0

Assume that k is 10 percent. The internal rates of return offered are: Project A, 25 percent; Project B, 22 percent.[17]

The net present values, at 10 percent, are: Project A, $910 and Project B, $1,116. Hence the relative ranking given by the two methods is in conflict. The rate of return approach would select Project A. The net present worth approach would select Project B. Why the difference, and which is correct?

The source of conflict can be isolated by comparing the relative values of the two projects, at some future point of time which lies beyond the terminal date of either project.[18] To do this we must make an explicit assumption about the rate at which funds produced by each project are reinvested.

The implicit assumption of those who believe the rate of return criterion is universally correct is that the appropriate reinvestment rate is the same rate as that earned by a project within its original economic life, i.e., its own internal rate. Given this assumption, it is clear that the project which has the higher internal rate of return will also have the higher accumulated terminal value, and hence the greater investment worth.

The implicit assumption made by those who believe the net present worth approach is universally correct is that the appropriate reinvestment rate is the cost of capital, k. Given this assumption the terminal values obtained will always rank the same way as present values.

The question of which method is correct can be resolved only

by deciding which assumption is more appropriate. In all but a
few exceptional cases, the generally accepted answer is that k is
the best available estimate of the reinvestment rate, i.e., the extra
flow of earnings produced in the early years by Project A will allow the company to invest funds it otherwise would not have had
only at the normal rate k. The logic of this is that the company
would invest anyway in all projects offering returns greater than
k and that the special gains available from these do not generally
depend on having the extra cash flow offered during earlier years
by Project A.

However, there may be some rare instances in which Project A
should be allowed a higher reinvestment rate than k. This is the
case if we postulate successor projects to Project A, which would
not exist in its absence. Here, the appropriate reinvestment rate
is the rate expected on these successor projects. In such a case
the question of whether alternative A or alternative B is the better
one must be resolved by making an explicit estimate of the reinvestment rates. If this is done the correct choice is that alternative which offers a larger accumulated terminal value. But apart
from these special instances, the general assumption used by the
present worth approach is the logically defensible one, and the
criterion of net present worth contributed by a course of action
provides a universally correct basis for investment decisions.

A rational investment policy requires that the new investment
budget should include all available uses of funds which promise to
create net present worth, i.e., which offer returns that have a present worth in excess of the outlays required to achieve them when
both flows are discounted at the company's cost of capital. When
two ore more courses of action are mutually exclusive, and neither
offers special reinvestment opportunities, the one which makes the
larger contribution to net present worth represents the correct investment decision. There will, of course, always be investment
opportunities for which estimation is quite impossible. A good example of these is investment in pure research. In this case a rational approach is not possible and it is necessary to fall back on
a subjective-judgmental basis for deciding how much should be
spent and in what way.[19]

NOTES

1. For a discussion of this form of financial analysis, see American Management Association, "How the DuPont Organization Appraises Its Performance," Financial Management Series: No. 94.

2. This could be negative, i.e., ongoing operations could require funds during a given period.

3. The problem of judging management effectiveness is outside the scope of this book. In general, there are two reasons for separating the evaluation of asset usage from the evaluation of managerial performance. First, the level of management being evaluated may not have the final authority over the amount of assets being charged to it. Secondly, the book values used in this kind of analysis, especially with respect to fixed assets, can be an extremely deceptive basis for judging managerial effectiveness.

4. The brevity of the treatment given ongoing operations does not reflect their lack of importance: the management of existing investments is clearly the most important aspect of the total management process. But it is also a great deal broader than the definition of financial management adopted in this book. Further, the financial aspects of managing ongoing investments have been thoroughly and adequately treated in the existing literature.

5. Recent interest in the subject of profitability measures dates largely from the publication in 1951 of Joel Dean's Capital Budgeting. Since then, and especially during the past five years, there has been a deluge of articles on this subject in accounting, financial management, and technical journals and an increasing treatment of it in standard texts.

6. For a detailed discussion of the payback period and its relevance as a measure of profitability, see Dougall, "Payback as an Aid in Capital Budgeting," The Controller, XXIX, 67 plus and Gordon, "The Payoff Period and the Rate of Profit," Journal of Business, XXVIII, 253-60.

7. See Gordon, "The Payoff Period and the Rate of Profit," Journal of Business, XXVIII, 253-60.

8. Hill, "A New Method of Computing Rate of Return on Capital Expenditures," Philadelphia Society of Business Budgeting.

9. Dean, "Measuring the Productivity of Capital," Harvard Business Review, XXXII, 120-30.

10. Bates and Weaver, "Your Next Capital Venture," Chemical Week, LXXX, 113-26.

11. Business Week, September 27, 1958.

12. See Kenneth L. Boulding, Economic Analysis (New York, Harper and Brothers, 1948), ch. 35-36.

13. J. M. Keynes, The General Theory of Employment, Interest and Money (New York, MacMillan and Company, 1936), pp. 140 ff.

14. The rate k is expressed in decimal notation and the point of time to which values are generally adjusted is the present. However, the equation can be rewritten in terms of any reference point of time and will yield the same solution.

15. See James H. Lorie and L. J. Savage, "The Problems in Rationing Capital," Journal of Business, XXVIII (October, 1955) 229-39; and Jack Hirshleifer, "On the Theory of Optimal Investment Decision," Journal of Political Economy, LXVI (August, 1958), 329-52. Both are reproduced in Solomon, ed., The Management of Corporate Capital. For an earlier generalized statement, see Samuelson, "Some Aspects of the Pure Theory of Capital," Quarterly Journal of Economics, LI, 469-96.

16. This assumes that the quality of earnings offered by the new proposal is the same as the general quality of earnings on existing investments.

17. Continuous compounding is used in this example.

18. In this case the two terminal dates are the same, namely, the end of year 4.

19. There is some evidence that companies in which research outlays are large are attempting to find ways to guide judgment in these matters through an objective analysis of past results.

XI. FINANCING DECISIONS

This chapter brings us to the last segment in our chain of thinking, the analysis of financing decisions which a firm faces in a given period. As far as the financing decision, or the set of financing decisions is concerned, we can take several estimates and expectations as given. These are: current and prospective conditions in the capital markets; the gross flow of earnings (cash throw-off basis) expected from operations during the period; net additions or reductions of working capital implied by the operating budget; and gross capital expenditures implied by investment decisions contained in the capital budget, or carried forward from previous capital budgets.

Given these estimates the set of financing questions which must be answered is:

1. How much of gross earnings should be paid as cash dividends during the period and how much retained?

2. How large should planned liquidity be?

3. How much external financing should be arranged for during the period and in exactly what form?

All are active decision variables and none can be treated as a residual matter to be passively determined by the other two. Their joint goal is the same as that outlined in our earlier discussion of optimal financial structure, namely, to maximize the market value of a company and to minimize its cost of capital. But in a dynamic context the problem has an added dimension. This is that it must take into account not just present conditions but the range of probable future conditions in the three major markets with which a company deals, i.e., products, labor, and capital. In other words, we are talking about maximizing market value not just at a single point of time but over all periods of time.

A unique "correct" solution for the entire set of financing de-

cisions probably exists but our understanding of the parameters
of the very large number of interrelationships involved is still too
small to permit the formulation of a truly general solution which
has operational meaning. In any case, such a solution has not been
put forward in the literature thus far and we will not attempt one
here. The best we can do in this final chapter is to sketch the components of the overall financing decision in terms of the major considerations that should be taken into account.

Dividend Considerations

In a world of perfectly rational investors and managers, dividends can be treated as a passive residual. In such a world, a firm
would invest the internal funds it generates either within the firm
or by acquiring assets of another firm, subject only to the constraint that each new investment has a net present worth greater
than zero, i.e., that the expected yield on internal investment is
higher than the capitalization rate for earnings of the quality expected. After all such investment opportunities have been ex-
hausted, any internal funds remaining would be distributed to
stockholders as cash dividends.

The assumptions here are that owners invest in a company in
order to maximize their own wealth; that acceptable internal or
external investments, as defined, offer rewards larger than the
individual owner can achieve for himself; and that owners who
choose to consume a part of their wealth can always do so by selling a fractional part of their holdings, presumably at a price which
continuously reflects the net present worth added by the process
of internal investment.

If the present system of taxation, with its lower rate on capital
gains, is superimposed on this pure model, the case for treating
internal investment as primary and dividends as a residual is
strengthened even further because, with taxation, the net yield
available on individual investment per dollar of dividend paid becomes even lower than the net yield available through retention
for internal investment purposes and the accompanying capital
gain.[1]

Some companies do follow the policy approach outlined above,
but the majority do not. The general practice is to treat dividends
as an active policy variable with retentions as a residual. Under
this policy, acceptable opportunities for internal investment which

cannot be financed by the residual flow of retained earnings are financed from external sources.[2] In a sense one could say that under such a policy dividend payments are financed from borrowed funds!

It is true that the practices of companies which adopt a positive dividend policy vary widely with respect to the average ratio of payments to earnings. Nonetheless the companies all share the belief that stable dividend payouts, gradually changed in the same direction as long-run earnings, come first. Whatever earnings remain are actively invested internally (along with external funds if this is necessary), or held in liquid form, or paid out as "extra" dividends clearly labeled as such, depending on the relation between the volume of planned investment and the volume of residual retentions available.

Which policy is correct: one that treats internal investment needs as the prior active decision with dividends, if any, as a residual distribution, or one that treats stable (slowly growing) dividends as an active decision variable with retentions as a residual? Or is it really a matter of indifference as far as the goal of net present worth maximization is concerned (assuming of course that all acceptable investment proposals and only acceptable investment proposals are always undertaken).

All three points of view have their adherents, in theory as well as in practice, although dominant practice is to treat the dividend payout as an active decision variable. Several kinds of argument can be made to support the ultimate "rationality" of the majority practice in the real-world environment within which business operates.

1. First is the ideological argument that the market should decide the reallocation of earnings to investment. By and large this is not a convincing argument unless one is also prepared to advocate a policy of 100 percent payout of profits and no net retentions.[3] Furthermore, as long as individual investors are free to buy or sell securities they can also change a company's cost of capital, and so long as internal investment policy is subject to this constraint the market can direct the share of real investment as between one firm and another.

2. A second argument is that the tax laws forbid and penalize "undue retention." This argument is also relatively trivial and

applies only to cases where retention is demonstrably for the purpose of personal income-tax avoidance.[4]

3. A third argument is that there are enough investors who have an irrational preference for dividends as opposed to capital gains; that these investors depend on dividends for spendable funds and that they are unprepared to exchange dividend receipts for an even greater amount of net spendable funds if this requires that they sell a fraction of their holdings. There can be little doubt that such investors do exist and that they regard expenditures of proceeds from dividend checks as infinitely more moral and appropriate than "dipping into capital."

But for every little old lady who thinks of her holdings of IBM (bought at 42) or Lincoln Life (bought at 71) as a disappointing part of her portfolio because if "doesn't pay dividends" one can also find investors who have exactly an opposite and equally irrational bias in favor of growth. Given this mixture of irrationality it cannot be assumed a priori that market values will be dominated by either.

4. We come therefore to the fourth and crucial argument, that stable, generous dividends are valued more highly than unstable, niggardly dividends (assuming no variation in the stability of earnings) and that a dollar of dividend is valued more highly than a dollar of net present worth (much more highly if tax-differentials are included).

One kind of evidence put forward in support of this proposition is that derived from cross-section statistical studies which show that the relation between observable market values and dividends is stronger than the corresponding relation between market values and earnings. An elaboration of this test puts both earnings (or retentions) and dividends into a single equation along with market values, and these also confirm the greater average influence of the dividend variable.[5]

But neither kind of test in itself confirms the proposition at issue. For one thing, the fact that current earnings (which is the form in which earnings are generally defined for statistical-testing purposes) may sometimes be negative whereas dividends are zero or positive and market values are always positive, imparts a significant bias to the results. But more important than this, dividends reflect long-run future earnings (the real determinant of market values) whereas current earnings do not. In other words, dividends have an important informational content and this, rather than the preference for cash dividends as such, is responsible for the stronger observed relationship between dividends and market values.[6]

These counterarguments cannot be ignored, and it is becoming clear that as far as the theoretical issue is concerned the question of dividends vs. earnings as a determinant of stock prices must be answered within the combined dividend and earnings framework put forward earlier in chapter V. According to this framework, market values can be stated either as a function of dividends plus growth or as a function of earnings plus net growth. Since net growth is equal to growth less an allowance for the reinvestment of earnings required to achieve that growth, both formulations, correctly stated, amount to exactly the same thing.[7]

But the issue we are now concerned with is whether the market, for whatever reason, rational or irrational, does or does not value one kind of dividend policy more highly than another. As far as this issue is concerned the evidence does support the traditional hypothesis that an optimal dividend policy does exist and that the kind of policy pursued can affect market value.[8] This may be due to the informational content of dividends. Or it may be due to the tangible evidence dividends provide that a company is able to generate cash. Finally it may be due to a general lack of faith in the market's ability to prevent wide prolonged departures of realizable market value from intrinsic values and hence to a preference for a stable dividend policy that does not require an investor to sell part of his holdings in each period for income purposes. All this might seem immaterial but the evidence clearly shows that it exists. One could argue that dividend payments or increases in dividend payments are an "expensive" means of communicating information to the market (expensive because of the personal tax liability and the expense connected with raising external funds to replace the outflow of liquidity from the firm). But in an uncertain world in which verbal statements can be ignored or misinterpreted, dividend action does provide a clear-cut means of "making a statement" that "speaks louder than a thousand words."[9]

In summary, argument on the dividend policy decision boils

down to a simple conflict between two views. One view is that it
does not matter in the least: given that investment policy is inde-
pendently determined, dividend policy is a mere detail which
makes no difference.[10] The opposing and more widely held view
is that dividend policy does matter and that one among the many
available decisions about dividends is superior to others. Given
the fact that dividend decisions always have an important informational content, the latter view must emerge as the correct one.

Any dividend policy can be described in terms of how steady
dividends are (or how steadily they grow) and the average ratio
of planned dividend payout to adjusted earnings.[11] An optimal answer to the second and more important question will depend on
two broad factors: the volume and quality of acceptable internal
investment opportunities and the volume of external, nonequity financing indicated by an optimal leverage policy.

In pragmatic terms, dividend policy formulation would follow
the following sequence: Company investment policy, based on the
systematic acceptance of all projects offering a yield higher than
the cost of capital, determines the gross volume of capital expenditures, C, to be made in a given period. Operating policy and the
projected operating budget provide an estimate of gross funds, Q,
available from operations (after taxes and fixed charges but before depreciation). In addition the operating cash budget implies
some increase or decrease, N, in net investment in inventories,
accounts receivable and other components of circulating capital.
Adjusted gross funds, Q − N, are available for reinvestment or
disbursement as dividends. Let M be the estimate of reinvestment
required to maintain capital assets intact, i.e., to maintain the
productive and earning power of the firm. In the absence of other
evidence, M will be equal to normal book allowance for depreciation.

In terms of these given factors, the broad financing policy decision involves, first, how much of new capital investment, C − M,
should be optimally financed by external debt sources and how
much by using internal funds from the amount Q − N − M which
is available. The optimal amount of leverage, L (discussed below)
depends on the market's evaluation of the size and stability of
Q − N − M and for present purposes we can take the leverage objective as given. Optimal dividend policy will depend on the rela-

tion between $(1 - L)(C - M)$, the portion of net capital expenditures to be financed with equity, and $Q - N - M$, the net flow of internal equity funds being generated.

If $(1 - L)(C - M)/(Q - N - M)$ is a small fraction, then a policy of high average dividend payment is indicated. The larger the fraction the lower the indicated payout, subject to the constraint that the amount of dividends paid should not decline below any "regular" dividend level already established. This approach suggests that firms with stable revenues, stable investment opportunities, long financial planning horizons, and inexpensive access to debt funds can afford to have a stable dividend policy and that they should adopt one because of the apparent preference of the market for such a policy. The optimal level of payout to be adopted will depend on the volume and quality of investment opportunity, the optimal use of leverage, and the volume and stability of internal fund generation expected. Given these conditions, a firm should pay regular dividends equal to the maximum it can expect to pay consistently. Quite possibly the indicated maximum may be zero. If no present policy exists this is entirely consistent with the objective of market value maximization. However, if past dividend policy does exist, this presents a further constraint that must be taken into account: either by changing the policy quite deliberately or, alternatively, by living with it even though this implies a less-than-optimal use of funds. None of this is very exact. Nor can we be more exact until we know more about the intricacies of investor preference and market valuation.

By and large the hypothesis is consistent both with the financial objective of market value maximization and with the behavior of firms. Large firms that can afford generous stable dividends do have such policies; firms that have a need for equity capital which is relatively high pay low but steady dividends. Finally, firms with highly variable revenue flows and variable investment opportunities, shorter planning horizons and relatively costly access to external funds, cannot afford to treat dividends as an active decision variable and tend to treat dividends as a residual.[12]

The Leverage Consideration

The maximum amount of leverage which "should" be used is limited for each firm by the point at which the marginal cost of borrowing exceeds the average cost of capital. The location of this point varies from industry to industry and from firm to firm and it depends largely on the attitudes, rational or otherwise, of those who provide the credit. These attitudes in turn are shaped broadly by traditional views on what is appropriate and in individual cases by lender expectations with respect to the stability of net revenues.

The traditional approach to financial analysis is too well documented to be repeated here. It consists of certain limiting ratios for various industries and industry groups, such as the ratio of debt to net worth; of fixed charges to available means of meeting them; of asset categories to liability categories.[13]

The economic analysis approach looks at the probable stability of operating earnings in terms of three major factors:

1. Expected fluctuations in national income and output. This is largely a matter of macroeconomic analysis.

2. Implied fluctuations in a company's sales and revenues. The principal guides here are the growth phase to which a company's product lines belong and the sensitivity of product prices and sales (income elasticity) to changes in national income and output.

3. Sensitivity of operating earnings to changes in the volume of output. This is primarily a matter of the firm's technological production conditions which determine the fixity of costs and the location of its break-even points.

The combined effect of all three elements determines the degree of expected instability in earnings. Given a firm's commitment to certain product lines and production methods this expected instability is also given. From the lender point of view, the amount of financial leverage or fixed charges a firm should be allowed to assume depends on the expected range of fluctuations in operating earnings. The more stable these earnings are, the higher the permissible amount of fixed charges, and vice versa.[14]

Finally, lenders also look at the average practice of other firms in the industry: financial structures which do not conform to standards of group performance tend to be suspect. These considerations shape bond ratings and credit ratings. They also set the limits of the use of leverage by any given company, either in the form of an absolute rationing of credit or in the form of a rapidly rising marginal cost of debt funds.

These limits represent the maximum extent to which a firm should borrow. The use of borrowed funds beyond these limits will reduce market value and raise the cost of capital. In any simple model, which assumes that earnings expectations are given, the maximum limit is also the optimum limit. The reason for this is that borrowing provides a tax benefit which accrues to stockholders and hence the greater the leverage the greater the benefit. But if we recognize that earnings expectations depend on average underlying expectations about the economy, the problem is no longer a simple one. Because the objective estimates of uncertain earnings are themselves subject to unmeasurable degrees of subjective uncertainty, optimal financing policy also requires a margin of security or safety as a protection against the remote contingency that possible, but improbable, outcomes may actually occur. As long as this consideration is present, the optimal debt structure will be somewhere below the maximum debt structure. In view of the subjective nature of the basic consideration, objective judgment on just how much below the maximum a firm should set its own debt limit is not possible. All we can talk about is how a firm would have performed if it had used borrowing differently over a given past period.[15] As a result of the subjective complications, no specific objective optimum exists for any given firm, and all we have is an optimum range running from no long-term debt whatever to a maximum level (well below 100 percent debt), which is imposed by the rising marginal cost of debt funds which a firm actually faces. Within this range, each firm selects its own level. And financing policy depends on the level selected.[16]

The Duration Consideration

Thus far we have ignored the fact that debt itself can be derived in many forms, which vary with respect to a number of factors. One of these is duration, the degree of permanence with which a firm commits itself to use borrowed funds and the corresponding degree of permanence with which the lender commits funds to the company. The problem of matching the duration of debt liabilities to the duration of the earning assets a firm intends to acquire through the use of debt funds is a significant consideration for financing policy.

In analyzing the effect of duration on the cost of debt funds it is necessary to recognize three components of cost. One is the rate of interest paid. Another is the length of time for which a commitment is made to pay this rate. The third is the "cost" of renewing short-duration loans, including the uncertainty of their renewal. At one extreme, long-duration borrowing (non-callable long-term bonds, for example) provide no renewal costs. But they commit the borrower to pay a fixed rate of interest for the entire life of the bond. Callable bonds allow more flexibility but carry a somewhat higher rate because of this. Short-term borrowing is the most flexible as far as duration is concerned but involves the cost and inconvenience of continuous renewal, at rates and terms that vary with the market. In addition, it exposes the firm to the possibility that a renewal may not be obtainable. The general recipe for achieving an optimal balance between these various considerations is that debt-structure should continuously be structured to asset structure, i.e., that fixed assets and "permanent" working capital should be financed with long-term liabilities and that temporary (seasonal or cyclical) working capital needs should be financed by temporary or short-duration sources. The logic of this rule of thumb is evident and needs no explanation.

However, the period-to-period interpretation of the basic rule is subject to considerations implied by financial or interest-rate forecasts held by financial management. Neither of these can be discussed except in a particular context of a given firm, and given and prospective conditions in the debt markets. Given these conditions, the translation of a firm's estimates into financing action with respect to duration is a fairly uncomplicated matter which does not involve conceptual difficulties.

Liquidity

One particular aspect of the duration problem is the question of how much liquidity to aim at in a given financing period. Unlike the duration problem proper, which seeks to match the duration of liabilities to assets, it requires matching the amount of a particular category of asset (cash and U.S. government securities) to current liabilities and prospective cash outflows.

The traditional approach to the liquidity question is to set it in terms of some "normal" ratio of current, or quick assets to current liabilities. This approach does not provide a guide to the optimal amount of liquidity that should be held but only to the minimum amount required. Even for the latter purpose it is not very satisfactory without considerable amendment.

One problem with the current-ratio, the most widely used meas-

ure for assaying liquidity, is that it compares two balance sheet
quantities. Since a balance sheet represents values at a given
moment of time, the measure is subject to whatever biases might
be involved in the particular closing date selected. For example,
if the observable current ratio is greater than unity, it would be
lower than the observed value if each of the following events had
occurred a day before rather than a day after closing date: a purchase of inventory on credit; the borrowing of short-term money;
the receipt of deferred income. On the other hand, some events
would raise the current ratio (originally greater than unity) if they
occur a day before rather than a day after closing: payment of
weekly or monthly payroll; repayment of a short-term loan; earning of "deferred income."[17] But more important than the vagaries
to which it is subject, a balance sheet ratio fails to measure liquidity specifically in terms of the protection it is designed to provide. Such a measure would require the comparison of the stock
of liquid assets held against the net outflows of liquid funds that
can be expected under various conditions.

Such an approach to the analysis of liquidity, or the defensive
position of a firm, must depend explicitly on cash-flow forecasts.
The first step would be to estimate the expected level and timing
of all cash outflows; namely, to construct a cash disbursement
budget. The second step would be to estimate the expected level
and timing of cash receipts over the same period of time. The two
forecasts provide a projection of what the cash position of the firm
will be for each point of time within the period, assuming the firm
begins the period with no cash. The largest negative position
shown by this forecast is the minimum inventory of cash or near-
cash (generally U.S. government securities) which a firm must
hold.

If conditions of absolute certainty prevailed this minimum required cash inventory would also be the actual liquid asset position that should be maintained by a firm. However, assuming there
is some uncertainty with respect to the cash receipt and disbursement forecasts, it is reasonable to maintain a "cushion" of liquid
assets over and above the amount implied by the transactions forecasts. It also seems reasonable to plan such a cushion in relation
to the forecast of cash or liquid asset requirements. Thus a
planned cushion might be measured as one that allows a company
to meet its liquid asset requirements for X days or weeks independent of any cash receipts. The number of days or weeks clearly

would depend on the probability of variation in the cash forecast, and on the opportunity cost of holding nonearning assets. On this basis the evaluation of the defensive or liquid position of a firm should be made by expressing the stock of liquid assets as a function of the projected need for liquid assets.[18]

Net Financial Position

Operating decisions with respect to credit the firm plans to grant and decisions made with respect to leverage, duration, and liquidity imply a certain overall relationship between a firm's stock of monetary assets (those with values fixed in terms of dollars) and its monetary liabilities. If monetary assets exceed monetary liabilities, the firm is a net creditor. If the reverse is true, the firm is a net debtor.

If the company expects the general price level to be stable, its net financial position as a creditor or debtor is not an important consideration. It is simply the passive by-product of other active decisions, and should be treated as such. But if a firm expects the general price level to rise or fall, then its net financial position does affect the future value of the equity holdings. As an illustration, take two firms A and B, with the following financial positions:

	Firm A (in dollars)	Firm B (in dollars)
Tangible operating assets	100,000	10,000
Monetary assets[a]	5,000	95,000
Total	105,000	105,000
Debt	20,000	60,000
Common equity	85,000	45,000
Total	105,000	105,000

[a]Includes cash, U.S. government securities, and accounts receivable.

Firm B is more heavily levered than Firm A and is more heavily in debt. But Firm B is a net creditor and it is Firm A which is the net debtor. Given a substantial (for example, 10 percent) but unpredicted rise in all prices, the conventional argument would be that debtors would benefit and that trading on the equity would produce advantages for the owners, i.e., that the owners of Firm B

would be better off than the owners of Firm A. But this is not so.
What happens depends on the net financial position and not on the
amount of debt or the amount of leverage as it is conventionally
measured.

With a 10 percent rise in prices, the tangible earning power of
both firms would presumably rise and this in turn would increase
the market value of the tangible operating assets held by each company. For simplicity, let us assume that this rise is also 10 percent. Thus Firm A's tangible assets would increase in dollar value
from $100,000 to $110,000. Since the dollar value of its outstanding
debt is unchanged, the equity holders will capture the entire gain
and equity holdings will enjoy a rise in value from $85,000 to
$95,000 or a gain of over 17 percent, and a net gain in purchasing
power.

Owners of the more heavily levered Firm B would actually lose
purchasing power because, in spite of their heavier debt and leverage position, their net financial position is that of a net creditor.
In the example given, B's tangible assets rise in value by 10 percent to a new value of $11,000. The dollar value of common equity
rises from $45,000 to $46,000—and since prices have risen by 10
percent, B's stockholders suffer a net loss in purchasing power.
B's gross debt position is more than offset by its greater holdings
of monetary assets.

The implication for financing policy is an important one:
Whether or not financial structure affects the value of a company
at any given point of time, it does have an effect on the value the
company will have over periods of time. In particular, if a general
price rise is predicted, net financial position acquires a position
of some importance as a criterion of financial policy, i.e., it ought
to be treated as an active policy variable, along with leverage, duration, and liquidity.[19]

The Timing of External Equity Financing

Thus far, the discussion has not said anything about the use of
external equity funds. Rather, we have analyzed the relative use
to be made of external debt and internal equity. So long as overall
investment and liquidity requirements can be met from these two
sources, the question of external equity issues does not arise. Nor
should it arise, because flotation and distribution costs alone make
external equity more expensive than internal equity. However, it

is likely that optimal uses of internal sources and of debt are not sufficient to provide the funds required by a company's internal investment opportunities. In this case the logical policy is to seek external equity financing through a new stock issue.

Unlike internal funds or external debt, external equity is not a source that can be tapped continuously or in small uneconomic amounts. The essential element in new equity financing once the need has been established is timing. And this depends upon the relation between a company's evaluation of what the value of stock should be in the light of prospective earnings and the net value actually placed on the stock in a given market. If the two coincide, the decision to embark on a stock issue is largely a technical one of exactly when, how, and through whom. If, however, actual net market values are below the company's evaluation of what they should be or what they are likely to be in the future, the company faces several alternatives: It can wait, and hence delay the execution of worthwhile investment projects which have been approved, or it can raise the funds in some other way, even though this might produce a financial structure that differs from the optimal one, and then later restore the desired financial structure through an external equity issue which is sold when market prices rise to levels justified by the company's estimate of earnings prospects.[20] A third way, which is a variant of the second, is to use the device of a convertible bond or debenture issue, with which the eventual elimination of debt liabilities takes place automatically.[21] A final alternative is to split off a large investment opportunity into a separate entity and to arrange for its financing on the basis designed to preserve existing stockholders' equity and control in operations that appear to offer opportunities for large rewards.

Can the various elements we have outlined be combined into a comprehensive theory of optimal financing? Probably not. As suggested earlier in this chapter, a unique "correct" solution for the entire set of financing decisions must exist, but our understanding of the very large number of interrelationships involved is still too small to permit the formulation of a general solution that has operational significance, even at the purely normative level.

Like the optimal set of investment decisions (the selection of assets), the optimal set of financing decisions (the selection of liabilities) can be defined as that set which maximizes the net present worth of the company in the light of the expected range of future developments. In the case of individual investment decisions, the operational prescription for a company is to accept an investment opportunity which offers a positive net present worth. Or, where two or more opportunities are mutually exclusive, to accept that set which offers the largest contribution to net present worth.

The corresponding prescription for financing decisions is harder to define and even harder to formulate as a measurable basis for action. In the first place any financing alternative or set of alternatives is one of many mutually exclusive alternatives available to a company. Hence it is always a question of choosing the best among competing possibilities. In operational terms, the best is that which maximizes net present worth.

If we look at the financing decision in itself, it is possible to reason in terms of the net present worth of an act of financing. This is equal to the present amount of liquid funds it provides less the estimated present worth of the cost it involves. This "cost" in turn is equal to the stream of incremental cash outlays required in the future because the financing act is undertaken, discounted at the company's present cost of capital plus an allowance for any fall in the net present worth of outstanding shares expected as a result of the new financing action. Thus, adding one dollar of short-term debt to the financial structure provides benefits equal to the net amount of funds received now (which may be less than one dollar) and has a cost equal to the sum of (a) the present value of the associated debt charges incurred, discounted at the company's cost of capital, and (b) the fall in the net present worth of shares associated with the increase of debt in the financial structure.

The problem of optimal financing is to find that set of financing alternatives which has the highest net present worth (in the algebraic sense). An alternative way of saying the same thing is that the firm should seek that form of financing which has the lowest marginal cost (including allowances for premiums or discounts as well as allowances for any loss or gain in the net present worth of outstanding equity debt claims on the company).

As stated above, there is a clear-cut conceptual parallelism between the task of optimal investment selection and optimal financing. The important difference between investment decisions and financing decisions emerges when we move from the conceptual level to the operational catergories in which each is stated. The decision to acquire an asset runs in terms of categories about which business has considerable accumulated experience and which can, therefore, be translated into numerical values. We do have some basis, although crude, for estimating incremental earnings, incremental costs, and incremental taxes associated with proposed investments. These estimates, together with an estimate of a company's cost of capital provide the operational guides required for the selection or rejection of an asset or the choice between two mutually exclusive assets.

In contrast the operational restatement of a financing decision, i.e., a decision to incur one kind of "liability" as opposed to another, involves categories for which we have very little accumulated evidence or experience as far as explicit numerical values are concerned. Neither the academician nor the businessman knows much about how to go about the task of measuring the net present worth of an act of financing. Such a measure requires knowledge of the basic capitalization rates for various kinds of claims as well as the expected change in each rate for every change in the mix of financing used. In short, it requires a level of knowledge about investor and lender reactions which we do not as yet possess.

In the absence of this kind of information and evidence, a formal statement of the optimal financing decision in operational terms must remain a relatively empty one. Nor can it be adequately filled except by empirical evidence on reactions of the capital market to risk, uncertainty, and profit. Until this is done, a comprehensive and meaningful theory of optimal financing decisions is not possible.

NOTES

1. The reader will recall from chapter V that the personal tax payable by owners on dividends received should not alter the minimum required return on internal investment.

2. The classic descriptive treatment of company dividend policy is by Lintner, "Distribution of Income of Corporations Among Dividends, Retained Earnings and Taxes," American Economic Review, XLVI, 97-113. See also Lintner's "Determinants of Corporate Savings," in Heller, Boddy, and Nelson, eds., Savings in the Modern Economy.

3. Obviously, during periods of inventory change and inventory price changes this must be adjusted to exclude "paper profits" or inventory profits which are tied up within the assets from which they emanate.

4. Section 102 of the old revenue code, and revised Sections 531-37 in the Internal Revenue Code of 1954. For an analysis see James K. Hall,

"Revision of the Internal Revenue Code and Section 102," National Tax Journal, VIII (September, 1955), 275-86.

5. There are a large number of studies which contain empirical evidence that dividends and payout ratios do matter. See, for example, Durand, "Bank Stocks and the Analysis of Covariance," Econometrica, XXIII, 30-45, and "Growth Stocks and the St. Petersburg Paradox," The Journal of Finance, XII, 348-63; Gordon, "Dividends, Earnings and Stock Prices," Review of Economics and Statistics, XLI, 99-105; Johnson, Shapiro, and O'Meara, "Valuation of Closely-Held Stock for Federal Tax Purposes: Approach to an Objective Method," University of Pennsylvania Law Review, C, 166-95; Harkavy, "The Relation Between Retained Earnings and Common Stock Prices for Large Listed Corporations," Journal of Finance, VIII, 283-97; and Walter, "Dividend Policies and Common Stock Prices," Journal of Finance, XI, 29-41.

6. For a statement of this kind of bias, see Modigliani and Miller, "The Cost of Capital, Corporation Finance and the Theory of Investment: A Reply," American Economic Review, XLIX, especially p. 667.

7. See chapter V, pp. 60-61.

8. For a straightforward but unproved assertion of the traditional position that a stable, generous dividend policy maximizes market value, see Benjamin Graham and David L. Dodd, Security Analysis, 2nd edition (New York, McGraw-Hill, 1940), chapter 29.

9. An announced change in the discount rate by the Federal Reserve Authority is another example of a so-called irrational means of communication which decision-making authorities are unprepared to give up in in favor of more verbal forms of communication. And there are many more examples of relative human sensitivity to tangible action and relative insensitivity to "mere talk."

10. Compare Modigliani and Miller, "The Cost of Capital, Corporation Finance, and the Theory of Investment," American Economic Review, XLVIII, 266: "As long as management is presumed to be acting in the best interests of the stockholder, retained earnings can be regarded as equivalent to a fully subscribed, preemptive issue of common stock. Hence for present purposes, the division of the stream between cash dividends and retained earnings in any period is a mere detail."

11. Reported earnings adjusted for nonrecurring profits or losses, e.g., inventory profits or losses, capital gains or losses, on asset disposition, the effect of "underdepreciation" or "overdepreciation" of fixed assets.

12. For discussions of financing practices by aggregative groups of firms, see Dobrovolsky, Corporate Income Retention, 1915-1943; Darling, "The Influence of Expectation and Liquidity on Dividend Policy," Journal of Political Economy, LXV, 209-24 and "A Surrogative Measure

of Business Confidence and Its Relation to Stock Prices," The Journal of Finance, X, 442-58; Lintner, "Determinants of Corporate Savings," in Heller, Boddy, and Nelson, eds., Savings in the Modern Economy; Tew and Henderson, eds., Studies in Company Finance; and Shapiro, "The Market for Corporate Securities: A Progress Report," The Journal of Finance, XII, 136-47.

13. For a discussion, see Roy Foulke, Practical Financial Statement Analysis, 3rd edition (New York, McGraw-Hill, 1953).

14. For a discussion, see Waterman, "Financial Leverage," in Essays in Business Finance, and Bellemore, Security Analysis.

15. See, for example, Foster, Corporate Debt and the Stockholder— The Effects of Borrowing on Rates of Return.

16. For a readable discussion of various corporate attitud s toward debt, see Silberman, "How Much Money Can Business Borrow?," Fortune, LIII, 131-35; and "The Fine Art of Raising Capital," Fortune, LIV, 96-99.

17. See Sorter and Benston, "Appraising the Defensive Position of a Firm: The Interval Measure," The Accounting Review, XXXV, 633-40.

18. This technique for measuring the liquid position of a firm is put forward in Sorter and Benson, "Appraising the Defensive Position of a Firm: The Interval Measure," The Accounting Review, XXXV, 633-40.

19. For a discussion of these ideas, see Kessel, "Inflation-Caused Wealth Redistribution: A Test of a Hypothesis," American Economic Review, XLVI, 128-41, and Kessel and Alchian, "Redistribution of Wealth Through Inflation," Science, CXXX, 535-39.

20. For evidence that the volume of new common stock financing by companies appears to reflect prices and conditions in the stock market, see Harold W. Stevenson, Common Stock Financing, Michigan Business Reports, Number 29 (Ann Arbor, University of Michigan, 1957), especially Chart 1, p. 7. Since periods of high stock prices tend to coincide with periods of high investment activity and hence with high needs for funds, it is possible that the observed timing of company financing reflects needs rather than cost conditions.

21. The use of convertible debentures by AT&T is an excellent example of this. See "12 Million New Telephones," Fortune, XLI (June, 1950), 81 ff.

CLASSIFIED BIBLIOGRAPHY

General Works

Dean, Joel. Capital Budgeting. New York, Columbia University Press, 1951.

Fisher, Irving. The Nature of Capital and Income. London, Macmillan Company, 1912.

_____The Rate of Interest. New York, Macmillan, 1907.

Gordon, Myron J. The Investment, Financing and Valuation of the Corporation. Homewood, Ill., Richard D. Irwin, Inc., 1962.

Solomon, Ezra, ed. The Management of Corporate Capital. Glencoe, Ill., The Free Press of Glencoe, 1959.

Williams, J. B. The Theory of Investment Value. Cambridge, Harvard University Press, 1938.

The Finance Function: Scope and Objectives

Anthony, Robert N. "The Trouble with Profit-Maximization," Harvard Business Review, XXXVIII (November-December, 1960), 126-34.

Calkins, F. J. "University Courses in Finance," The Journal of Finance, IV (September, 1949), 244-65.

Dauten, Carl A., et al. "Toward a Theory of Business Finance," The Journal of Finance, X (May, 1955), 107-43.

Glover, J. D. The Attack on Big Business. Boston, Division of Research, Harvard University Business School, 1954.

Gordon, R. A., and James E. Howell. Higher Education for Business. New York, Columbia University Press, 1959.

Halley, D. M., et al. "Materials and Methods of Teaching Business Finance," The Journal of Finance, V(September, 1950), 270-92.

Harris, D. W. "The Financial Executive's Part in Management,"

in Financial Executives' Series: No. 1. New York, American
Management Association, 1925.
Hunt, Pearson. "The Financial Policy of Corporations," Quarterly
Journal of Economics, LVII (February, 1943), 303-13.
McKinsey, J. O., and S. B. Meech. Controlling the Finances of a
Business. New York, Ronald Press, 1923.
March, James G., and Herbert A. Simon. Organizations. New
York, John Wiley and Sons, 1958.
Margolis, Julius. "The Analysis of the Firm: Rationalism, Con-
ventionalism, and Behaviorism," Journal of Business, XX
(July, 1958), 187-99.
Mason, Edward S. "The Apologetics of Managerialism," Journal
of Business, XXXI (January, 1958), 1-11.
Pierson, Frank C. The Education of American Businessmen. New
York, McGraw-Hill, 1959.
Robbins, Sidney, and Edward Foster, Jr. "Profit-Planning and the
Finance Function," The Journal of Finance, XII (December,
1957), 451-67.
Sutton, Francis X., et al. The American Business Creed. Cam-
bridge, Harvard University Press, 1956.
Upton, R. Miller. "Conference on the Teaching of Business Fi-
nance," The Journal of Finance, IV (September, 1949), 243.
Voorhies, Darrell H. "The Treasurer and the Controller," in Lil-
lian Doris, ed., Corporate Treasurer's and Controller's Hand-
book. Englewood Cliffs, N.J., Prentice-Hall, 1950.
Weston, J. Fred. "The Finance Function," The Journal of Finance,
IX (September, 1954), 265-82.

The Cost of Capital

Durand, David. "The Cost of Capital, Corporation Finance, and
the Theory of Investment: Comment," American Economic
Review, XLIX (September, 1959), 639-54.
_____ "The Cost of Debt and Equity Funds for Business: Trends,
Problems of Measurement," in Conference on Research in
Business Finance. New York, National Bureau of Economic
Research, 1952.
_____ "Growth Stocks and the St. Petersburg Paradox," The Jour-
nal of Finance, XII (September, 1957), 348-63.
Gordon, Myron J., and Eli Shapiro. "Capital Equipment Analysis:
The Required Rate of Profit," Management Science, III (Oc-
tober, 1956), 102-10.

Lanzillotti, Robert F. "Pricing Objectives in Large Companies,"
   American Economic Review, XLVIII (December, 1958), 921-40.
Lintner, John. A New Model of the Cost of Capital: Dividends,
   Earnings, Leverage, Expectations and Stock Prices. Unpub-
   lished paper presented at the annual meeting of the Economet-
   ric Society, December, 1960, St. Louis, Missouri.
Mayer, Robert W. "Analysis of Internal Risk in the Individual
   Firm," The Analysts Journal, XV (November, 1959), 91-95.
Modigliani, Franco, and M. H. Miller. "The Cost of Capital, Cor-
   poration Finance, and the Theory of Investment," American
   Economic Review, XLVIII (June, 1958), 261-97.
_____ "The Cost of Capital, Corporation Finance, and the Theory
   of Investment: A Reply," American Economic Review, XLIX
   (September, 1959), 655-69.
_____ Leverage, Dividend Policy and the Cost of Capital. Unpub-
   lished paper presented at the annual meeting of the Economet-
   ric Society, December, 1960, St. Louis, Missouri.
Morton, W. A. "The Structure of the Capital Market and the Price
   of Money," American Economic Review, XLIV (May, 1954),
   450-54.
Solomon, Ezra. "Measuring a Company's Cost of Capital," Jour-
   nal of Business, XXVIII (October, 1955), 240-52.
United States Federal Communications Commission. Federal
   Power Commission re Transcontinental Gas Pipe Line Cor-
   poration. Docket No. G-1277, April 28, 1950.
_____ Michigan Public Service Commission re Michigan Gas and
   Electric Company. Docket No. 1103, March 5, 1950.
_____ The Problem of the "Rate of Return" in Public Utility Regu-
   lation. Washington, D.C., United States Government Printing
   Office, 1938.

Investment Decisions and Capital Budgeting

Bates, Alan G., and James B. Weaver. "Your Next Capital Ven-
   ture," Chemical Week, LXXX (June 15, 1957), 113-26.
Bierman, H., and S. Smidt. The Capital Budgeting Decision. New
   York, Macmillan, 1960.
Dean, Joel. "Measuring the Productivity of Capital," Harvard
   Business Review, XXXII (January-February, 1954), 120-30.
Dougall, Herbert E. "Payback as an Aid in Capital Budgeting,"
   The Controller, XXIX (February, 1961), 67 ff.

Gordon, Myron J. "The Payoff Period and the Rate of Profit,"
Journal of Business, XXVIII (October, 1955), 253-60.

Hill, Horace G., Jr. "A New Method of Computing Rate of Return
on Capital Expenditures," Philadelphia Society of Business
Budgeting, 1953.

Lutz, Friedrich, and Vera Lutz. The Theory of Investment of the
Firm. Princeton, N.J., Princeton University Press, 1951.

McLean, John G. "How to Evaluate New Capital Investments,"
Harvard Business Review, XXXVI (November-December, 1958),
59-69.

Matthews, John B., Jr. "How to Administer Capital Spending,"
Harvard Business Review, XXXVII (March-April, 1959), 87-99.

Samuelson, Paul A. "Some Aspects of the Pure Theory of Capital,"
Quarterly Journal of Economics, LI (May, 1937), 469-96.

Financing Decisions and Financial Structure

American Management Association. "How the DuPont Organization
Appraises Its Performance," Financial Management Series:
No. 94. New York, 1950.

Bellemore, D. H. Security Analysis. New York, Simmons-Board-
man Publishing Company, 1959.

Darling, Paul G. "The Influence of Expectation and Liquidity on
Dividend Policy," Journal of Political Economy, LXV (June,
1957), 209-24.

_____"A Surrogative Measure of Business Confidence and Its Re-
lation to Stock Prices," The Journal of Finance, X (December,
1955), 442-58.

Dobrovolsky, Sergei P. Corporate Income Retention, 1914-1943.
New York, National Bureau of Economic Research, 1951.

Durand, David. "Bank Stocks and the Analysis of Covariance,"
Econometrica, XXIII (January, 1955), 30-45.

Eiteman, W. J. "Promotion," Essays in Business Finance. 3d ed.,
Ann Arbor, Mich., Masterco Press, 1957.

Foster, Louis O. Corporate Debt and the Stockholder—the Effects
of Borrowing on Rates of Return. Hanover, N.H., Amos Tuck
School of Business Administration, Dartmouth College, 1956.

Gordon, M. J. "Dividends, Earnings and Stock Prices," Review
of Economics and Statistics, XLI (May, 1959), 99-105.

Harkavy, Oscar. "The Relation Between Retained Earnings and
Common Stock Prices for Large Listed Corporations," The
Journal of Finance, VIII (September, 1953), 283-97.

Johnson, L. R., Eli Shapiro, and J. O'Meara. "Valuation of Closely-Held Stock for Federal Tax Purposes: Approach to an Objective Method," University of Pennsylvania Law Review, C (November, 1951), 166-95.

Kessel, Reuben A. "Inflation-Caused Wealth Redistribution: A Test of a Hypothesis," American Economic Review, XLVI (March, 1956), 128-41.

Kessel, Reuben A., and A. A. Alchian. "Redistribution of Wealth Through Inflation," Science, CXXX (September, 1959), 535-39.

Lintner, John. "Determinants of Corporate Savings," in Heller, Boddy, and Nelson, eds., Savings in the Modern Economy. Minneapolis, Minn., University of Minnesota Press, 1953.

——"Distribution of Income of Corporations Among Dividends, Retained Earnings and Taxes," American Economic Review, XLVI (May, 1956), 97-113.

Nielsen, Scott. Market Value and Financial Structure in the Railroad Industry. Occasional Paper No. 4, Hartford, Conn., Travelers Insurance Company, March, 1961.

Porterfield, J. T. S. "Dividends, Dilution and Delusion," Harvard Business Review, XXXVII (November-December, 1959), 56-61.

Schwartz, Eli. "Theory of the Capital Structure of the Firm," The Journal of Finance, XIV (March, 1959), 18-39.

Shapiro, Eli. "The Market for Corporate Securities: A Progress Report," The Journal of Finance, XII (May, 1957), 136-47.

Silberman, Charles E. "The Fine Art of Raising Capital," Fortune, LIV (July, 1956), 96-99. Reproduced in J. F. Weston, Readings in Finance from Fortune. New York, Henry Holt and Company, 1958.

——"How Much Money Can Business Borrow?," Fortune, LIII (June, 1956), 131-35. Reproduced in J. F. Weston, Readings in Finance from Fortune. New York, Henry Holt and Company, 1958.

Sorter, George H., and G. Benston. "Appraising the Defensive Position of a Firm: The Internal Measure," The Accounting Review, XXXV (October, 1960), 633-40.

Tew, Brian, and R. F. Henderson, eds. Studies in Company Finance. Cambridge, England, Cambridge University Press, 1959.

Walter, James E. "Dividend Policies and Common Stock Prices," The Journal of Finance, XI (March, 1956), 29-41.

Waterman, Merwin H. "Financial Leverage," in Essays in Business Finance. 3d ed. Ann Arbor, Mich., Masterco Press, 1957.

INDEX